BEGIN FISHING
WITH
UNCLE BILL

D1434699

By the same author:

* THE FISH WE CATCH
* FRESHWATER FISHING
* SEA FISHING
* PLACES TO FISH IN BRITAIN AND IRELAND
  FLY DRESSING AND SOME TACKLE MAKING (Fully
     bound)
  SALMON AND SEA TROUT FISHING
  TROUT AND GRAYLING FISHING

* Also available in *paperfront* editions, uniform with this
  volume.

BEGIN FISHING

WITH

UNCLE BILL

Written and illustrated

by

W. E. (BILL) DAVIES

Contributor to:
"Chasse et Pêche," Brussels, "Angler's World", "Trout and Salmon",
"Irish Stream and Field", etc.

PAPERFRONTS

ELLIOT RIGHT WAY BOOKS
KINGSWOOD, SURREY, U.K.

Made and printed by Love & Malcomson Ltd., Redhill, Surrey.

CONTENTS

		Page
Introduction	. . . .	11

FRESHWATER FISHING SECTION

1. Tackle for Freshwater Fishing	. . .	14
2. Fish Haunts and Useful Baits	. . .	22
3. Float Fishing	. . . . . .	30
4. Pike Tactics and Baits	. . . .	56
5. Grayling—Silver Lady of Winter	. . .	69

GAME FISHING SECTION

6. Trout	. . . .	76
7. Sea Trout	. . . .	99
8. Salmon	. . . .	109
9. Fly-dressing Know-how	. . . .	128

SEA ANGLING SECTION

10. Sea Angling	. . . .	138
11. Collecting Your Own Baits	. . .	150
12. Deep Sea Fishing	. . . . .	162
13. Beware of these Fish	. . . .	178
14. Sea Angling Homework	. . .	182
Index	. . . .	190

LIST OF ILLUSTRATIONS

			Page
Fig.	1.	Goose quill float	16
„	2.	Balsa wood float	17
„	3.	Elder pith float	19
„	4.	Fish haunts in a river	23
„	5.	Spoon and worm combination	25
„	6.	Wet fly and nymph	29
„	7.	Weight for plumbing depth	31
„	8.	No. 16 Crystal bend hook baited with bread paste	32
„	9.	No. 16 Crystal bend hook baited with maggot which lies in hook bend	34
„	10.	Easy to make perch paternoster	35
„	11.	Wine-bottle minnow trap	37
„	12.	Celluloid funnel for jam-jar minnow trap	39
„	13.	Making quill minnow	41
„	14.	A carp lake showing likely fishing spots	49
„	15.	Outline sketches of rudd and roach	52
„	16.	Tackle for barbel	54
„	17.	Live rudd on snap tackle	58
„	18.	Three items of tackle when pike fishing	59
„	19.	Artificial baits	65
„	20.	Anti-kinks	66
„	21.	Pike paternoster	67
„	22.	Grayling float for worm or maggot	71
„	23.	Grayling lures	73
„	24.	Winged wet- and dry-flies and spider	82
„	25.	Wet spider flies and nymph	83
„	26.	Line loop and knots	85
„	27.	Double three-fold blood knot	86
„	28.	Worm on Pennell tackle	95
„	29.	Natural baits	97

Page

Fig. 30. Natural baits 101

„   31. Sea trout flies 105

„   32. Salmon worm hook 113

„   33. Natural baits mounted 115

„   34. "Otter" 118

„   35. Balsa-wood Devon 119

„   36. Dry-flies for salmon 125

„   37. Half-hitch and whip-finish knots . . 129

„   38. March brown spider (wet) . . . 130

„   39. Mallard and claret sea trout fly . . 132

„   40. The Black Ghost 133

„   41. Wet and dry hair-wing flies . . . 135

„   42. Blue Charm salmon fly 137

„   43. Estuary sea trout fly on No. 8 hook . . 145

„   44. Flounder spoon 147

„   45. Mussels and cockles 152

„   46. Limpet baits 154

„   47. "Sand-eels" 157

„   48. Using a squid as bait 159

„   49. Pennell tackle for tope 165

„   50. Drift-line tackle 169

„   51. An easily made ledger tackle . . . 170

„   52. Nylon paternoster 172

„   53. Rauto plaice spoon 175

„   54. Flowing trace tackle for bream . . 177

„   55. How to make mackerel and pollack spinners 183

„   56. Wire clips for weights 185

„   57. An easy made wire trace 187

„   58. Perspex boom 188

INTRODUCTION

SOME of the happiest days of my life were those during which I was engaged in the task of educating my son and two daughters into the art of angling in its many forms and phases. Through their eyes and reactions I relived my own youth, a period now more than half-a-century away. Some years ago I had a nephew and niece as pupils, and now my grandson is taking his first steps towards becoming an angler.

One of the most difficult things I have found when teaching younger people is trying to curb their natural impatience. However, patience is the keynote to all forms of teaching and it is also the keystone to success in all types of angling whether it be freshwater, game or sea fishing. The person who is always in a hurry, never stopping to think as to why this or that happens, will never make a good angler. An old angler wishing to pass on knowledge to a younger generation finds it difficult.

Of course any instructor attempting to teach an art—and angling is an art—through the written word, must necessarily confine himself to general methods that will fit the average person. Explanation of each step can be fully detailed, but these details must follow a concise pattern that makes no allowance for differences of personality or of adaptation. To do otherwise would merely mire the beginner down in a morass of technicalities that would probably cause him or her to give up in disgust. Once the rudiments of angling in fresh or saltwater are absorbed, beginners usually develop a technique of their own. That is the goal of every instructor.

However, the novice who eventually becomes an expert in whatever type of angling he ultimately takes up seriously will invariably be the individual who becomes a

11

keen student of Nature in all her variable moods. This is because weather conditions and temperature of air and water affect fish no matter what their habitat, more than we even in this "Enlightened age" realise.

One might think that after more than two thousand years of angling we ought to know something about fish, but, frankly our knowledge is only slight. Long before Moses scratched the Commandments on tablets of stone, fish were succumbing to the lure of man-made tackle, flies and spoons. I have no doubt that two thousand years from now it will be the same.

Casting and the care of tackle are mechanical things that can be taught to anyone, but the expert angler is invariably one who has developed an inquiring mind and is observant at all times. On stream and lake, every day brings its problems and the solutions usually lie in simple matters, such as observing what is happening and why it should be so. Of course there are occasions when despite one's knowledge of fish behaviour the answers are not forthcoming, that is as it should be. If we caught a large number of fish each time out angling would never have retained its appeal to both young and old.

Today most young people have minds that are highly developed, moreso, I believe, than in my generation. The educational methods of today are directly responsible for this. Young people are taught to inquire into this and that and observation develops automatically. As a result problems that would have taken me, when a youngster, some time to figure out are with the present generation dealt with speedily and logically.

To make for easy reference the book is divided into three parts, Freshwater fishing (I detest the word "Coarse" for there is nothing coarse about it), Game and Saltwater. In every chapter there will be sketches and diagrams of items of tackle any teenager can make for himself, for believe me there is always an added thrill and attraction when you land a fish on some piece of equipment you have made yourself. Looking back over the years I remember the thrill it gave me when I landed a small gudgeon on a spade-end hook I had whipped myself. As the years went by I learnt how to make my own freshwater rods and later how to dress flies. I think the greatest thrill of all was when my first salmon was landed on a fly made by myself. It was a Blue Charm and roughly made though it was, it caught a fish and that was all that mattered so far as I was concerned. Today the Blue Charm is still a favourite of mine. What is more it is a very simple pattern to dress. There is a chapter on fly-dressing but in so brief a compass I can tell you only how to dress one or two flies. However the method is very much the same for all.

1

Tackle for Freshwater Fishing

BEFORE dealing with the principal methods of catching various species of fish that inhabit river, lake and canal it might be just as well to mention the tackle required, but I shall keep it to the barest minimum. This means that all one requires for the initial outfit is a rod, reel, line, three floats, hooks and split shot (weights), landing net and keep net and also a rod rest and a disgorger for removing hooks from fish.

In the old days rods were made out of a variety of woods including cane, lancewood and greenheart, and a good many anglers used to make their own. As a matter of fact the first "bottom-fishing" rod I ever owned was a whole cane one with a light greenheart top. It was 9ft. in length and was made for me by my father for fishing bread paste, worms and maggots. It was top-heavy, but it caught fish so I was happy. My rod rest was a forked stick cut from the hedge. A few years later my parents presented me with a Hardy rod which I still possess.

ROD-KITS

Today most tackle-makers sell what are known as rod-kits and with one of these any intelligent boy or girl can make up their own rod with very little trouble.

On the Hampshire Avon the other day I watched a boy of nine years catch roach and dace on maggot as well as many an adult. His rod was a nine feet long hollow glass twopiece he had made himself from a rod-kit.

In these days the emphasis is on light tackle. I think that hollow glass is best for not only is it exceedingly light, but it is also most serviceable. Another big factor is that it is unaffected by damp, the arch-enemy of built-cane rods. However, to keep the rod looking spick and span it should be given a rub down with a soft cloth after each outing. In a later chapter care of tackle will be fully dealt with.

FIXED SPOOL REEL IS BEST

Experience leads me to the opinion that a fixed spool reel is best for the beginner. Lifting a bail-arm on such a reel is a much more simple operation than "thumbing" a centre-pin or multiplyer reel, and there is less danger of an over-run ("bird's nest" some people call them and on occasions they certainly look like a nest) when the line is in tangled coils. Of course when this happens valuable fishing time is lost and occasionally one loses both temper and patience. So take my advice and invest your money in a fixed spool reel. Such a reel for boy or girl is inexpensive. As one's angling education advances more expensive equipment can be purchased.

MAKE YOUR OWN FLOATS

In regard to floats, the one my father started me off with was a six inch porcupine quill and even after all the years that have sped by since then, I still think it is one of the best floats ever invented. Today like most things associated with fishing tackle the newcomer is faced with scores of different types of floats in all manner of shapes and sizes. However, if handy with tools it is a fairly simple matter to make your own out of goose or swan quills, cork or balsa wood. Most tackle shops stock balsa wood float blanks, already drilled, which can be purchased for

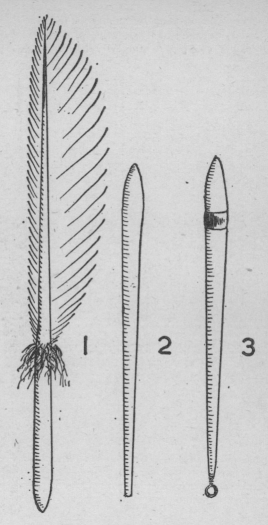

Figure 1. Goose quill float.

1. Goose wing feather.
2. Six-inch length of quill has been stripped.
3. The finished float complete with float cap.

a few pence. They are usually in six inch lengths.

All that is required to be done is for a piece of cane or a quill to be given a coating of glue and then pushed

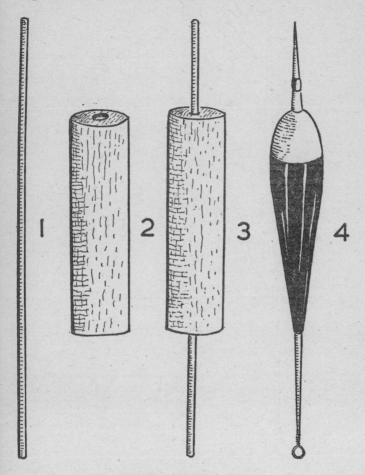

Figure 2. Balsa-wood float.

1. Six-inch length of cane.
2. Three-inch piece of balsa.
3. Balsa is glued on cane.
4. The completed float.

through the hole. When set the blank can be shaped with fine glass paper then given a coating of model aeroplane dope to seal the fibres. When dry your float can be painted the desired colours. Today one can get fluorescent paint and this shows up much better at a distance than ordinary paint or enamel. Use such colouring for the top half of the float and ordinary paint for the section that will be submerged when in use. (See Sketch).

Cork floats can be made just as easily from ordinary bottle corks that can be purchased at any chemist's shop. With cork one has to drill through the centre of the corks first. This can be done with a nail (suitable size of course) that has been made red-hot. Held with a pair of pliers the nail will make a nice neat hole. The procedure is then the same as previously described.

The eye at the end of your float can be made out of light gauge copper, brass or stainless steel wire and whipped on with fine nylon sewing thread. The float-cap, that little gadget which fastens the line to the float can be made out of bicycle valve tubing. A six inch length of tubing will make at least a couple of dozen caps. Of course the time will come when you will want a selection of different sized caps; these can be obtained from most tackle shops, and are usually made of plastic which is more durable than rubber.

ELDER PITH FLOATS

Another material for float-making is elder pith. A friend of mine who is a dedicated roach angler makes his floats out of this material.

He tells me that the summer is the best time to get in a supply of pith. Select those branches that are straight and with bright green skin which indicates new growth. When you get home cut them into six-inch lengths and put them in the sun to dry. It is then an easy matter to strip with a fine bladed pocket-knife the thin wood covering thus exposing the white pith. The best sized pith to work with is from three-quarters to one inch diameter.

After the wood has been removed leave the pith in the

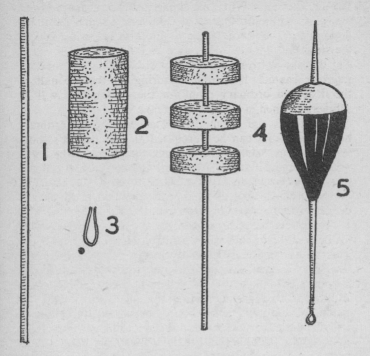

Figure 3.   Elder pith float.

1. Five-inch length of cane.
2. Two-inch piece of elder pith.
3. Half-inch length of fine wire for eye.
4. Elder pith cut into discs, drilled, glued and put on cane.
5. A finished egg float.

sun for another three or four hours, by which time all moisture will have been removed. You are now ready to start float making and for this you will need a darning needle, a sheet of fine glass paper, a tube of glue and a piece of cane or a quill for the centre pin of the float.

Cut the six-inch length of pith into half-inch discs and put a hole through the centre of each just large enough to take the cane or quill. Each disc is given a coat of glue, top and bottom, pressed together and left to set for 24 hours. At the end of that time you can begin shaping your float with the fine glass paper. When shape and size have been achieved put on an undercoat of grey paint and when this is perfectly dry the finished colouring can be applied.

So when you are out for a walk during the summer keep a sharp look out for suitable elder and then those non-fishing hours can be put to excellent use.

HOOKS

Hooks are after all the connecting links, as it were, between angler and fish. There will always be arguments as to what is the best type of hook to use for this or that sort of fish. Be that as it may the newcomer will not go far wrong if he starts off with eyed hooks. They are much easier to change than spade-end hooks to nylon, what is more they are not so expensive. The science of hook-making has progressed rapidly in recent years and many different patterns are now on the market. I still prefer the Crystal hook above all others for roach, dace, chub, rudd, bream and gudgeon and Round bent hooks for perch and barbel. The hook sizes most used today for the fish mentioned range from No. 8 to No. 18.

It is quite possible that the novice may like to try spade-end hooks at some time or another. These can be purchased already whipped to nylon.

SPLIT SHOT

Most tackle dealers have on sale containers with compartments holding the various sizes of split shot one will normally use during a day's fishing.

FISHING LINE

When you purchase your reel be sure and get a spare drum for it so that you can have at your disposal a light line of two, three or four pounds breaking strain for roach, dace and rudd fishing on one drum and a six or seven pound line on the other for chub, bream and barbel fishing. Of course if you decide to go after pike you will want a much heavier line. There are many brands of nylon lines on the market with some much better than others. The softer the nylon the better it is in use, so it is always advisable to find out from a seasoned angler which is the best sort. Never hesitate to ask for advice. Believe me most anglers take a delight in putting a youngster on the right road. If there is a fishing club near your home join it as soon as you can, for then you will be able to obtain information from the local experts.

LANDING AND KEEP-NET

A landing net will be needed for the occasion when you hook a fish too large to land otherwise. There are all sorts and sizes, but select one with a long handle, for the time will surely come when it will be worth its weight in gold, for you will be able to reach a fish that would otherwise have broken free. The one I use has a collapsible handle, which when fully extended is five feet in length. Some of my friends have handles on their nets that are as much as nine feet in length.

Lastly a keep-net. Eventually the novice may enter competitions and then such an item of tackle is most essential. Here again advice from club members as to the best type to purchase is valuable. I entered my first competition when 12 years of age, thoroughly enjoyed it and received half-a-crown as the sixth prize-winner. I never did win the junior cup of my club, but I had some enjoyable outings during the years I competed.

All the species of fish mentioned in this book would require a book each to deal with them fully, so this work must be looked upon as a primer.

2

Fish haunts and useful baits

ONE of the major difficulties facing the novice on his first trip to a river is finding possible feeding places of the species he proposes going after. Of course float tackle, bait and technique for one kind will often do for another. But it is always well to remember that like humans, fish have their likes and dislikes; some species are gregarious, others prefer a lonely existence. However, each and every one will make a home in a place which promises the most food and protection from enemies.

The experienced and observant angler can with very little study select a place that is likely to produce what he is after. This ability to read and assess the possible potential of any water only comes with years of experience, but there are short cuts to such knowledge and a

---

Figure 4. Fish haunts in a river

1, 2 & 3. Roach are usually near weed beds.
4 & 5. Large perch like holes near bank.
6. Mouths of little feeder streams are good for chub.
7. Deep runs near and among weed are favoured by pike.
8. Fast water over clean gravel is liked by dace and grayling.
9. Eddies and runs near bankside rushes may hold chub, roach and dace.
10. Barbel like deep water over a gravel bottom.
11. Bream and tench prefer slow, sluggish water over mud.

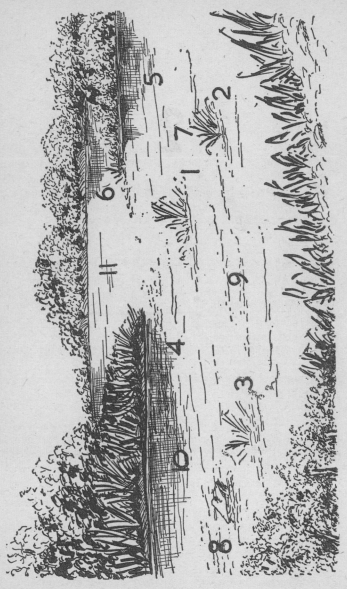

study of the accompanying sketch should help.

Taking roach first let us look more closely at this business of finding good places (swims). Main diet of this fish is insects, larvae and small crustacea, so where you have weed beds you will invariably find roach. Loving company, they move about in schools, so once you have caught one you can start to really enjoy yourself trying to lure some of his relatives.

In Hampshire, where I reside, we have two very famous roach rivers, the Avon and Stour: both have plenty of weed life and an abundance of roach as well as most other species including game fish. Indeed, the Avon is considered to be about the finest mixed river in the country.

The ambition of most roach anglers is to catch a two pounder. In all my years of fishing I have only managed to catch such specimens on two occasions, mind you I have come very near many times. Large roach prefer the quiet, more slow-moving reaches of a river, where there is both depth of water and shade from trees or bushes. Small roach inhabit water that is moving fairly fast. Baits that will entice roach, no matter what size include: maggots (gentles) bread-paste, bread cubes and flake, small red worms, stewed wheat and hempseed.

The same type of water and baits favoured by roach also suit rudd. During summer months rudd can also be lured with size 16 artificial flies and nymphs.

PERCH

In the search for roach swims one usually comes across deep holes, where the banks have been under-cut by fast currents and places where there are sunken tree roots with a deep hole scoured out behind them. Large perch delight in such places. The small and medium-sized ones are usually located in more shallow places providing it is shaded by bushes and trees. Small perch are voracious feeders and take worms and maggots as fast as you can bait up. The big chaps are a little selective at times, but when on a feeding spree can often be tempted by a lively worm, active minnow or gudgeon. Occasionally they will

24

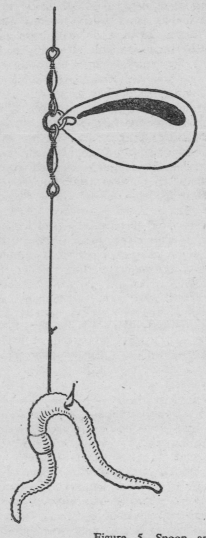

Figure 5. Spoon and worm combination.

strike at artificial baits such as the spoon or devon. I have often taken perch of two pounds on a combination of spoon and worm (see illustration). Such spoons are easy to make and how to set about making them is described in chapter 10, page 148.

described in chapter 10, page 148.

CHUB

This strong fighting fish, like the roach, is an insect and larvae feeding variety, but also likes such things as caterpillars, cherries, elderberries. bread-paste, cheese-paste, bread cubes, bread-crust, minnows and can be lured to strike at such artificial baits as flies and spoons.

Gregarious, they move around in schools and prefer shaded streams and pools, weed-beds and fast runs between weed-beds, also eddies formed by rocks and other under-water obstacles. If when looking around you find a small stream that feeds the main river it is fairly safe to assume that periodically you will find chub nosing around where the waters meet.

TENCH

This is a bottom-loving fish and likes those areas where there is plenty of mud and weeds with plenty of depth. The best specimens are usually found in lakes. Like the chub it is a strong fighter. Baits include worms, maggots and bread-paste.

BARBEL

Next to the pike this is the largest kind of fish one is likely to meet in a river. A most powerful fighting fish it likes water that has plenty of movement, gravel bottom and weeds. It is a fish that likes a mixed diet, sausage meat, worms, maggots and bread-paste have all lured double-figure specimens.

The Hampshire Avon is one of our most famous barbel waters, and anglers from all over the country visit this water every year to pit their skill against it.

DACE

This is a sprightly little fish and delights in those places where there is a fast stream over a gravel bottom. An insect and larvae feeder it also likes maggots, worms, bread-paste and can also be lured with small artificial flies and nymphs.

GUDGEON

A bottom feeder this small fish is usually caught by anglers to be used as live bait for pike or perch. It likes those places where the water is very slow moving, maggots and small red worms are the usual baits.

BLEAK

Nearly a century ago the bleak was a most famous money-making fish, millions were netted from the River Thames and other waters and exported to France. Their scales were used in the manufacture of artificial pearls. It is a fast biting little fish and once a school of bleak moves into a swim the best thing the angler can do is gather up his tackle and move off elsewhere. If you want to do a little pike or perch fishing a two or three inch bleak makes an ideal bait.

EEL

Some of my friends fish for nothing else but eels because they love to eat them. Considered to be one of the most nutritious of fish practically every river and lake in the country will at some time during the season carry its quota of eels. Worm or a bunch of worms are the usual baits and night-time is considered the best period of all to go after the big ones.

GRAYLING

Although classed as a fresh-water fish it belongs to the salmonoid clan. It inhabits only a few of our rivers and these are generally well oxygenated waters with chalk or gravel bottoms. The river Test, famous for its trout is over-run with them and all manner of methods have been used to reduce their numbers so fast do they breed. They come into season in October and are excellent table fish. Baits include maggots, worms, bread-paste and artificial flies and nymphs.

PIKE

Many times in the past, this, our largest river fish has often been called the "poor man's salmon" due no doubt to the hard fight it puts up for its freedom when hooked.

It likes fairly deep slow-moving water in which there is plenty of weed life wherein it can hide while waiting for a meal to come along. This could be anything from ducklings, water voles or fish. Anglers' baits are usually live gudgeon, bleak, minnows, rudd and roach. Large specimens have also been taken on dead baits such as herring and sprat. Today many fishermen do not bother with natural bait preferring to use artificials such as large silver or gold spoons, wood and metal devons.

COMMON BREAM

This is a fish that likes very slow-moving water and some of the best fishing has been on the Thames, and Tring Reservoirs. Moving around in large schools, they can be caught on maggots, worm and bread-paste and many anglers, particularly in the Midlands use all manner of ingredients when making up their paste. A very dear friend of mine uses bread-paste in which he puts honey, and he catches large numbers.

CARP

This species is found in some of our more slow-running rivers, but they thrive best in lakes where there is plenty of weed life, water lilies and rushes.

Feeding principally on vegetable matter, worms, crustacea and larvae, the baits of the angler include mag-

Figure 6. Wet-fly and Nymph.
1. Wet-fly dressed on No. 14 down-eyed hook.
2. Nymph dressed on No. 16 down-eyed hook.

gots, caterpillars, worms, bread-crust and bread-paste. It is one of our most cunning fish and fights very hard when hooked.

OTHER SPECIES

There are other species of fish but the ones already referred to are the ones likely to be met with on most rivers. Of course rarely will any two waters hold the same varieties due to the prevailing conditions of both the water and locality. However the advice given as to conditions the various species like will be found to apply to most waters. There will always be exceptions to the rule for the simple reason that we are dealing with living creatures. A place that produced fish one day may be deserted the next. Why this should be is often a mystery to even the most expert angler, but it is this uncertainty that keeps an angler observant and in a frame of mind to experiment with baits and localities whatever type of water he happens to be fishing.

3

Float Fishing

Now that we have got rid of most of the preliminaries, we can start to think about the job of trying to catch fish. As in the previous chapter I propose to deal with roach first as the same techniques apply to the luring of a number of other species.

The roach is well distributed throughout England and Wales, not so widely in Scotland and found only in a very few Irish waters. It is a fish that probably, each week-end during a season, gives more sport to anglers than any other kind. However, like so many other varieties it likes a free "handout" from the angler. In other words ground-baiting is often the keystone to success. So before leaving home we have a couple of simple tasks to do, mix some ground-bait and then some paste for the hook.

GROUND-BAIT INGREDIENTS

The ground-bait I invariably use when paste is on the hook is made with the inside portion of a stale white loaf of bread. The bread is broken up into crumbs, the finer the better, and then mixed; two parts bran to one of bread. The ingredients are placed in a polythene bag and on arrival at the fishing venue it is moistened with water from there. Don't make it too moist, the idea being to make it just heavy enough when squeezed into a lump the size of a walnut, so that it will reach near the bed of the swim before disintegrating. The small particles will attract the fish without feeding them.

Regarding paste take no notice of the tales you hear about making it more alluring by adding essences of this and that flavour. Plain bread paste has proved its worth over the years and is still the best. Here's how to make it: First see that your hands are perfectly clean. Then take the inside out of a white loaf of bread, add a little water and knead the mixture until a dough-like consistency is reached. Put the dough in a polythene bag to keep moist and we are ready for the trip.

Arriving at the water, the first thing we do after arranging our seats and bits and pieces is to assemble the rod and then plumb the depth, so that we can fix the float at the depth we decide upon. With the water so slow moving today we will keep the bait about six inches from the bottom. Of course if no bites are forthcoming at that depth it is a simple matter to lower the float thus raising the hook or vice versa.

Figure 7. Weight for plumbing depth.

We now know the depth, but before we make our first cast a lump of ground-bait is tossed in just up-stream from where we hope the float will land, near to the weed bed a few yards from where we are. While the ground-bait is doing its job of luring a few fish into that locality a pellet of paste is pinched on to the No. 16 Crystal hook we are using as a start. The float is a porcupine quill and to "cock" it, keep it upright in the water, a couple of small split shot are nipped on eight inches from the hook. If there had been a strong current we should have needed a float that would have carried larger weight to counteract the pull of the current.

Figure 8. No. 16 Crystal Bend hook baited with bread-paste.

HOW TO CAST

The bail-arm of the reel is lifted and the line is held to the rod butt with the fore-finger, the rod is brought to the side and then smartly forward, at the same time the fore-finger is lifted as the rod faces forward and the tackle shoots ahead to the spot selected. A turn on the handle brings the bail-arm back into position, slack line is taken up and the rod is placed in the rest.

Sitting down we watch the float for any tell-tale quivers or other movement. If no bite comes after half-an-hour we flip in another lump of ground-bait. Periodically we reel in and examine the bait and if needed a fresh pellet is put on.

The first bite comes after a long wait and the fish, a six-inch roach is led away from the weeds, the net is slipped under and he is ours.

Right you have your first fish, the next job is to remove the hook, which I always do while the fish is in the net. We are often told to wet our hands before removing the hook from the fish, but I am afraid that more fish are harmed this way than are ever saved, for the simple reason that being slippy we tend to grip them too hard and internal injuries result. In my method the fish is handicapped in movement by the net and it is a very simple matter to retrieve the hook and release the fish.

If it is of good size the angler may wish to have it weighed for a possible prize, that being so it is put in the keep-net. If the fish is not of specimen size take my advice and release it at once. There is nothing more cruel, in my opinion, than keeping a lot of small fish in captivity. I appreciate that in match fishing it has to be done, I have done it myself on scores of occasions, but at the moment we are fishing for fun. There is no big cash prize at the end, but if you release the small fish as you catch them, you will at the end of the day have a sense of satisfaction in knowing that you have behaved like a true sportsman.

But to return to the job in hand. So far our paste has not produced anything very big, the half-dozen roach we have caught have all been about six inches so the time has arrived to try maggots. Hook and terminal tackle is the same, but before we bait the hook with one maggot we put in our ground-bait about a dozen of the smallest maggots. These will be released as the ground-bait breaks apart while sinking. Our cast is made and in a very short time we have a little larger roach, one of eight inches which keeps us occupied for a few seconds before the net curbs his activity. No good to keep, so in the water he goes. Some anglers believe that returning fish as you catch them alarms others in the swim, I have never found it so.

Figure 9. No. 16 Crystal Bend hook baited with maggot which lies in hook bend.

MORE GROUND-BAIT

Before another cast we throw in some more ground-bait. A few more small roach come to the net so a change of technique is indicated; ledgering might be the answer. This can be done with a float to indicate bites, minus the float one relies on the rod tip to indicate customers at the bait, however I much prefer "Touch ledgering" in which you hold the rod all the time. With this method even the most delicate nibble is felt. A "swan" shot is put on to keep the bait on the bottom, the bait is in position and we cast out, again near the weed-bed, where there is a lovely little eddy as the water sweeps round.

With ledgering one has to exercise to its fullest extent the virtue of patience. Sometimes the bait is taken quickly, very often you have to wait an hour or more before a fish shows interest.

Fortunately on this occasion we have not long to wait, a slight vibration is felt, the rod tip dips and the line moves slowly, the rod is lifted smartly, the line tightens

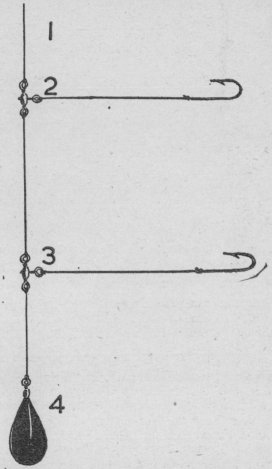

Figure 10. Easy to make perch paternoster.
1. Line to reel.
2 & 3. Two-way swivels with snoods and hooks attached.
4. Half-ounce Arlesey bomb weight.

and away goes the fish. Not a roach because he is "running" too hard. We play the fish back and just below the surface we see what it is, a nice little chub of about two pounds. Too small to keep, so back he goes, maybe to tell his friends of his strange experience, and so ends your first day as an angler. There will be many more, but if you are like me you will always remember the thrill of catching your first fish, so deeply will it be etched on the memory.

There are many variations in the use of float tackle and also the ledger, but once the rudiments of the more simple methods are mastered, the others follow automatically. By watching more experienced anglers your education rapidly advances until the day will come when you can hold your own in whatever company you may be fishing.

LURING THOSE BIG PERCH

A fish I never tire of pitting my skill against is perch, not the little chaps of a few ounces to a pound, but those voracious individuals of two pounds and over. During my career I have caught a good many three pounders in this country from river and lake, but my best specimens, three four pounders came from Loch Awe (Scotland) when spinning a two inch gold devon for trout near Kilchurn Castle, a tumbled-down ruin.

Now while perch can be taking on spinning baits, when I am going after these beautifully coloured fish I usually rely on paternoster tackle, two hook, which is easily made at home. The bottom hook is baited with worm and the top one has a sprightly minnow on. The worm is hooked in the normal way and the minnow is impaled through the back at the rear of the dorsal fin or through the top lip.

Figure 11. Wine bottle minnow trap.
1. Strong cord round clear glass wine bottle for tethering to bankside.
2. Bottle cork with hole through middle to allow free flow of water.
3. The glass "button" has been removed to allow access for minnows.
4. Crumbs of bread to attract minnows.

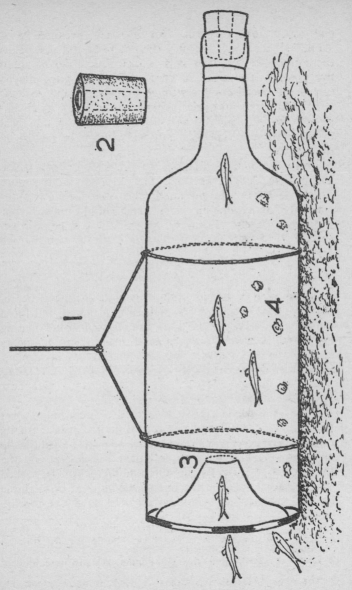

Worms are fairly easy to come by from old compost and manure heaps, but minnows require a trap of some kind or another. I use two types of trap and here again these are simple to make at home.

The first is made out of an ordinary wine bottle, see sketch. The button of glass at the bottom of the bottle is tapped carefully out using a poker or other blunt-ended piece of metal and a hammer. No doubt you will break a bottle or two in the process, I did at first, but eventually you will get the knack of how much strength to use with the hammer. A hole is also drilled in the cork to allow easy flow of water through the bottle. A couple of loops of strong cord are put on the bottle, pulled tight and then connected to a piece of string, long enough so that it can be pegged to the bank while the trap is on the bed of the river. Before lowering your bottle, take out the cork and put in a few small pieces of white bread, these will entice the minnows in.

If you place your trap in a good place it will only be a matter of minutes before you have a dozen or more nice baits. Take the cork out of the bottle after you have lifted your trap, select a minnow of two or three inches long, put the rest in the bottle and return it to the water. You now have a bait that has caught more specimen perch than any other.

The other trap I sometimes use is made out of an ordinary two pound, glass jam-jar and a funnel of celluloid. Two or three holes are drilled in the base of the jar with a masonry drill to allow flow of water. The funnel is fastened together with brass-headed paper clips, three tongues of celluloid are fastened to the funnel in the same way and then kept in place on the mouth of the jar with a strong rubber band. The tethering string is put on in the same way as the bottle trap.

If you do not want to be bothered making your own you can purchase from most tackle dealers traps made out of plastic, but as I said earlier one always gets an added thrill out of making something that aids in the capture of a nice fish.

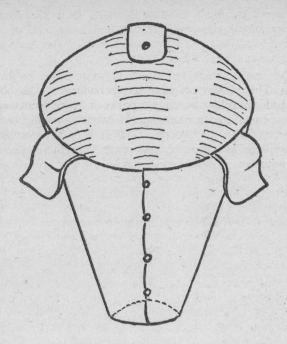

Figure 12. Celluloid funnel for jam-jar minnow trap.

When perch reach two pounds and over they have a tendency to lead a lonely existence. They set up house in some fairly deep hole and remain there until caught by an angler or die of old age. But each and every good perch hole I have ever discovered has always been near where smaller fish travel, this means that the perch is always assured of a meal and he does not mind if it is one of his own species so long as it appeases his hunger.

Some anglers use ledger tackle for perch and manage to catch some fine fish but I have always done best with the paternoster the weight on which is an Arlesey bomb. When the paternoster sinks out of sight with its double offering you may be in for a long wait, but if a perch is in residence it won't be that long before the frenzied antics of both worm and minnow have intrigued him so much that he comes out to investigate. The first indication of a bite will be a violent vibration of the rod top and then away will go the line. When the line stops moving is the time to lift the rod smartly to drive in the hook. Perch have a habit of carrying the bait a good distance in their mouth and striking as they are moving off with it will just pull hook and bait away from them, so exercise a little patience and barring accidents the fish will be yours.

SMALL SPINNERS ARE BEST

If you don't receive any offers to the paternoster then a little spinning might attract a nice fish, but keep the artificials on the small side. A spinning bait that has served me well on a few occasions is the quill minnow and one about two inches, coloured blue and silver or brown and gold is ideal. Chub and also trout are partial to this bait and on a couple of occasions I have caught small pike with it.

Quill minnows are easy to make at home and large wing feathers from geese and turkeys are excellent for the job.

Fifty years ago the quill minnow was considered to be one of the best artificials for perch, trout and sea trout, but over the years plastic substitutes and other lures have appeared until today it is not so popular among the younger generation of anglers. However, anglers of the old school know its worth and still use it. For my part I consider it to be one of the best all round artificials particularly for perch.

A three-inch one is the ideal size for perch so here is how to make them. Apart from the quills you'll need some eight pound breaking strain Alasticum wire, small swivels, tapered shank treble hooks, plastic tubing from used ball-point pens (use a pipe cleaner to get rid of surplus ink) and some celluloid for the spinning vanes.

Remove the fibres and soft fluff from the quill and cut to size then insert the plastic tubing after giving the outside a coating of clear nail varnish so that it will stick

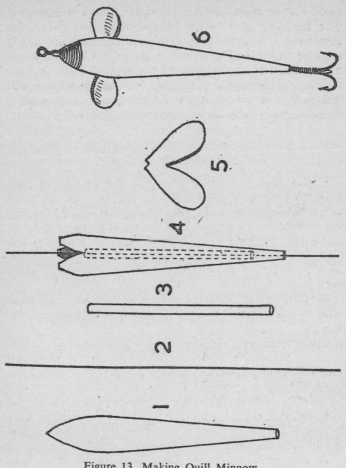

Figure 13. Making Quill Minnow.
1. Prepared goose quill.
2. Length of wire.
3. Plastic tube.
4. Plastic tube and wire inside quill.
5. Spinning vane ready for twisting.
6. The finished minnow ready for painting.

to the inside of the quill. The treble hook is whipped to
one end of the wire with fly-tyer's silk and given a couple
of coats of nail varnish. While it is drying, cut some slits

41

in the broad end of the quill, put your wire through so that the hook makes a nice snug fit and whip on a small swivel. It is then ready for the spinning vane which you have previously cut to shape. Twist this so that it has the appearance of an aeroplane propeller. Hold it in the steam from a boiling kettle with a pair of tweezers and twist with a pair of pliers and a dip in cold water will set the shape.

Before finishing off the head put in four or five dust shot so that the minnow will sink slowly at the end of a cast before the retrieve is started. The space still left at the head is filled with plastic wood smoothed into a neat shape and the notches are bound down with fly-tying silk.

You can paint the bait to represent an immature dace, rudd or roach, but leave the underside in its natural colour. When the paint on the back is perfectly dry give the whole minnow a coating of clear copal varnish.

Some quill minnows I have seen offered for sale have a couple of additional trebles, one near the middle of the body and another near the head, but from experience one treble at the tail is best.

If you follow the sketches step by step you should experience little difficulty when making your first one. After that it will be plain sailing.

WAYS WITH CHUB

From a sporting point of view, chub are excellent but are no use for the table, being full of small "V" shaped bones. On a summer evening fly-fishing for them takes some beating, but the majority of large chub are lured with paste, bread-crust, maggot and worm and live insects on float tackle. Before dealing with float-fishing we will look briefly at fly-fishing, because sooner or later you will have the urge to pit your skill against this gamester, using an artificial fly.

Chub flies are usually of the Palmer type, or in other words they have a cock hackle wound from one end of the shank to the other. The two patterns I rely on are the Black and Red Palmers. Chub love shady areas such as under trees or bushes that over-hang streams and pools. Many anglers use wet flies to lure chub, but I much prefer dry flies, and being well-hackled, Palmer flies float much better than most. In the old days we used all sorts of grease to make our flies float, but today a floatant for flies comes in a little can, you press a button and a fine spray of chemical compound which includes silicone covers the fly, which will then float for a considerable time without another annointing.

As to the technique of casting a fly we will deal with that in a later chapter. Of course a number of other fresh-water fish can be lured on an artificial fly and also nymphs, as I have already mentioned.

PASTES FOR CHUB

On the Avon we have some very large chub and each season a good number of five pounders are caught on paste made out of ingredients such as "high-smelling" cheese, boiled macaroni and cheese, bread-paste and cheese and ordinary bread-paste. My best fish have always come when I have been using bread and cheese-paste on a No. 8 or a No. 10 Crystal hook. Years ago the only Crystal hooks you could purchase were spade-ends but nowadays you can get them with eyes, which are much better when dealing with a hard-fighting fish like a chubb. No matter how good the whipping on a spade-end hook might be there is always a danger that it will strip under pressure.

Your float will be a little larger than that used for roach as it will have to balance a much larger knob of paste and possibly a swan shot. The first thing you should do after tackling up is look for signs of feeding chub. When feeding near the surface they usually betray their presence by sending out widening ripples on the surface of the water, but bear in mind that this species is noted for its good vision so keep out of sight as much as possible when you start fishing.

When chub show little interest in pastes it is a good idea to change over to maggot, impaling two, three or even six on the hook and some of the biggest ones I have seen have been lured by coloured baits, particularly maggots. The colour they seem to prefer is orange-red.

From a chemist's shop purchase some Chrysoidine dye and dissolve it in boiling water. Wait until cool and then bottle it. When required for use place a tea-spoonful of the liquid in a tin or other container and add bran, allow this to soak up the dye. Put in your largest maggots and keep them in the colouring until the required tint is obtained. Then take them out and put them in another container filled with dry bran.

Pastes can be coloured by putting in a little of the dye during the kneading process.

COLD WEATHER CHUB

In the winter months chub depart from their summer quarters and take up residence in the deeper pools, there to remain until warmer weather prevails. However, it is very rare for them to lose their appetite.

If you are on a strange stretch of water look for a place where the water drops off sharply from the bank. Chub like such places.

During periods of high water they prefer quiet back-waters out of the main current. They are friendly fish and move around in schools and it is quite possible when once they are located for an angler to take several before the school moves off.

However, while float tackle will produce good sport on most occasions some very big chub, fish of six and seven pounds have been taken on ledger tackle with a lively worm as bait. No self-respecting chub will pay attention to an inert worm lying on the bottom, but let that bait be a good wriggler, and of good colour as worms can be, and then it presents a meal the fish is loath to refuse. Keep your worms cool and in a container filled with damp moss and they will keep happy for a couple

44

of days, then it is best to release them and stock up with another lot. Worms can be difficult to obtain, both in very dry weather and also hard frosty periods, so in a later chapter I have written how to make your own worm farm. With this you are assured of an ample supply the whole year through.

SOME THOUGHTS ON BREAM

In bream fishing, more so, I believe, than in any other branch of angling, ground-baiting is a necessity, and this should be done, if possible, at least 24 hours before the actual fishing commences. One angler of my acquaintance gets a small pail of worms from a farm dung heap (the total number of worms must run into thousands) and dumps the whole lot into the place he has decided to fish. The next day he does not start fishing until late afternoon and I have never known him have a bad outing.

Frankly that is overdoing the job. A good overnight ground-bait is not whole worms, but worms that have been chopped in half and mixed with ordinary ground-bait.

When I lived in London one of my favourite venues for common (bronze) bream was Tring Reservoirs, in Hertfordshire. The local anglers when ground-baiting cut large turves and place a large number of worms on top of these and in a very short time the worms have burrowed inside the turf, they then sink the whole lot in the selected swim. While I have seen some good bags taken from a place so treated my personal experience of this method is nothing to write home about.

Ledgering with worm or plain bread-paste often lures a good fish or two, but my preference is float fishing, with the bait a few inches off the bottom. In this type of fishing it is not an uncommon occurrence to see the float come up and lie flat on the water and on numerous occasions I have seen anglers lose their fish by striking. What happens is that the fish takes the bait and rises with it in its mouth, the bait is nine times out of ten jerked out of its mouth. A much better method is to be patient, and in less than a second the float will start on its downward journey. Then is the time to strike and not before, because the fish has turned and the hook invariably lodges in the corner of its jaws. A second or two later and the hook will penetrate somewhere at the back of the throat. The disgorger will have to be used to remove it, and if care is not taken with this operation it will mean the death of the fish.

LARGE SCHOOLS

Bream move about in large schools and by using plenty of ground-bait they can be kept in the vicinity of the float. However, during a high wind float fishing is sometimes a problem. A float rising and falling with the waves spoils any chance of success. The bait behaves in a manner exciting the suspicions of the fish, and will therefore be left alone. Under such conditions it will be found that a long rod will give better line control than a short one, a fine line, say five pound breaking strain presents less resistance than a stouter one and the less of the float above water the less there is to catch the wind.

The aim must be to keep the float in the place you want it to be, so the terminal tackle must be "shotted" more heavily and carry a suitable float. Often it is advisable to nip on half-a-dozen split shot so that only the tip of the float is left above the surface. Many such floats have their tips coloured red, but I have found that bright yellow is much superior to all other colours.

Where you have a school of small bream of half-a-pound to two pounds, two or three maggots often proves an appetising lure. A friend of mine who fishes the Thames colours his maggots a deep yellow and he has won a number of competitions with such baits.

THOSE MUD-LOVING TENCH

A lover of quiet waters where there is an abundance of weed and mud the tench is most active during the warmer months of the year, as soon as the temperature drops it becomes torpid and buries itself in the mud staying there for days on end. For some years I had a large fish pond, so was able to study the habits of quite a number of fish, and the tench always intrigued me. I had half-a-dozen and during daylight they were rarely seen, but at dusk they put in an appearance, stirring up the mud and foraging among the weeds and marginal plant life.

The nocturnal feeding habits thus indicates the best time to try and lure one or two. Izaak Walton in his "Compleat Angler" says "He will bite at a paste made of brown bread and honey or a lob-worm." I have tried both these baits when fishing the waters of the Christchurch Angler's Club, Hampshire, of which I am a member. Both baits on a ledger tackle have proved their worth and it is rarely that I resort to anything else.

LONG-HANDLED NET

As a bite indicator a piece of silver paper was twisted on to the line so that I could see it, and as soon as it jerked I lifted the rod from the two rod rests, which held it in an horizontal position and was thus ready to strike. He is a determined fighter and the localities favoured by tench make landing a good one, say four or five pounds, a difficult job. A landing net with a five or six-feet handle is often a necessity and the terminal tackle should never be less than five pounds breaking strain.

Another bait with which I have had much success is the common water-snail, colonies of which can be found among the bank-side plants. Remove the shell and impale on a No. 8 or No. 10 Model Perfect hook, indeed my largest specimen to date, a fish of $5\frac{3}{4}$ pounds fell to its lure. Maggots have never proved very successful for me, although some of my friends have done exceedingly well with them.

While most of my best tench have come from lakes, quite a number of good fish have been recorded from slow moving rivers and canals, but by and large if you want to try your skill and patience with large ones your best chances, I believe, will always be on a lake.

A word of advice. Don't take your radio sets with

you, the less noise the better chance you have of a good fish.

COMMON CARP

This is another species that loves, mud and weeds, has nocturnal feeding habits and delights in quiet lakes with plenty of shade. Many anglers after years of fishing for carp consider them to be the most cunning of freshwater fish; maybe that is why I have never caught a really big one. My largest from a private lake is only 12 pounds, a baby when you consider that the record stands at 44 pounds.

In this lake which I fish quite often, are carp well over 20 pounds. But I have never been able to tempt one of these to take my bait. Of course there is always tomorrow.

It is not important, but it is still interesting to note that common carp were introduced into this country around the 12th century and were used by monks for stocking ponds, for use as food. On the Continent it is still used as such.

During the summer months carp like to bask just under the surface, but I have yet to hear of anyone catching one when it is so engaged and, as with tench, the best time to fish for them is during the hours of darkness. Where a water is known to contain twenty-pounders the terminal tackle should never be less than 10 lbs. breaking strain, the hook should be a No. 6 or No. 8 Model Perfect and your net should have an extra large mouth. When hooked a carp puts up a most determined fight, taking line off the reel in sharp bursts of speed and to net even a ten pounder at night is exciting and full of thrills due to the weeds and other natural obstacles you will have to bring him through. You may have to use a torch, but try and refrain from letting its rays shine on the water.

PATIENCE IS NEEDED

The carp fisher must be imbued with an abundance of patience and he may go to the water several nights before he connects with a fish. I well remember spending a whole

Figure 14. A carp lake showing likely fishing spots.
1. During daytime carp like to browse and bask among and near weed beds.
2. Deep water near shaded banks is a favourite place.
3. Near lily pads and bush-shaded banks are also favourites.
4. At night-time carp come close to shore to forage among weeds and rushes.

week on a well-stocked carp lake near London without so much as a bite, the following week a friend of mine fishing the same swim and using the same sort of tackle and bait caught four, one being 18½ pounds. Carp are like that, you just never know when they are going to co-operate with you.

Baits I have used with a fair amount of success include, bread-paste, plain bread-crust, fruit cake, worms, beetles and maggots. Touch ledgering will sometimes get a customer or two, but by and large it has been my experience that float tackle, with the bait a few inches off the bottom is the best. During winter carp vanish from their summer haunts and lie either in deep mud holes or among the rotting weeds. I have yet to tempt one after October, although a friend of mine has caught them on honey and bread-paste as late as December.

Two other varieties of the common carp are the leather and mirror. The former is almost scaleless and the latter has one or two rows of very large scales along its sides. On the Continent fish breeders many years ago by selective breeding from the mirror and leather carp developed what they call the "King" carp. It grows rapidly and to a great size. In concluding this piece on the common carp I must point out that when fishing for them you will need a powerful rod. There are quite a number of inexpensive hollow-glass rods on the market today that are excellent tools for the job, having flexibility and back-bone.

WAYS WITH DACE

It is difficult to reflect upon dace fishing without evoking memories of summer, for these sprightly little fish, the record is 1 lb. 8 oz. 5 grms., are most active during that period of a year. Some of the happiest days of my youth were spent sitting among tall clumps of foam-like meadow-sweet and willow-herb watching my float as it danced along a little stream in North Wales, near my home. Long-trotting, it is called, and on some occasions my bait, a single maggot, travelled 30 yards before I caught a fish.

Streamy waters not too deep and with a nice gravelly

50

bottom are the places to look for and from experience long-trotting is one of the best methods I have used. Of course you occasionally come across them in more quiet water. My largest dace was a fish of 12 ounces, taken from the North Tyne in Northumberland.

In the streams they will be found near the bottom, where they feed on nymphs, shrimps, grubs, etc., in those stretches containing weed they usually feed near the surface grabbing the insects as they float by. The most effective float comprises a slim six-inch porcupine quill with an oval-shaped cork body. About one-inch of quill should protrude above the cork and be painted bright yellow, as should the top half of the cork. The underside of the cork you can paint green and also the rest of the quill which should be about two inches. Such a float is easy to make at home.

However, to get the most sport out of the dace there is nothing, in my opinion, to beat fly-fishing for them. They will take dry-flies, wet-flies and nymphs and usually put up as good a fight as a trout of similar size. The flies, however, should never be larger than No. 16 which is the same size hook that I use when long-trotting with the single maggot. The leader (cast we used to call it) has to be fine, say tapered from four pounds breaking strain to one pound when using a dry-fly, and five pounds to two pounds when using wet-fly or nymph.

Many anglers stick to the old method when after dace which is bait fishing with maggot, small worm or paste. But when there is a nice hatch of flies they would, I am sure, have more fun if they learnt to cast a fly. Of course it means buying a fly-rod, but hollow-glass fly-rods are inexpensive these days. There are thousands of fly patterns, but the angler after dace should use the more sombre-hued flies, such as March Brown, Dark Olive, Black Palmer and Black Spider.

The line should be of the floating kind with a plastic covering, which does away with having to grease the line to keep it afloat. The same line will do for wet-fly and nymph fishing, providing you do not get any grease on your leader. How to cast a fly will be dealt with later on.

In habits this species is not unlike our old friend the roach and is often mistaken for roach. Indeed in Ireland where many waters abound with them they are often referred to as roach. However, to assist young readers here is an outline sketch of a rudd and a roach with the points to look for.

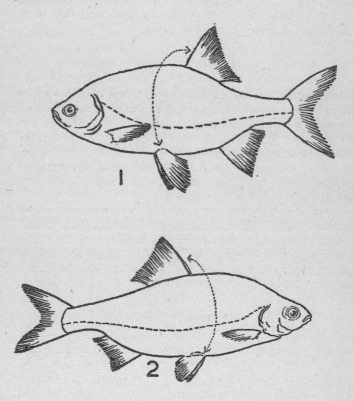

Figure 15. Out-line sketches of rudd and roach
1. Rudd, the dorsal fin of which is behind the ventral fins. The iris of a rudd's eye is yellow-orange.
2. Roach, the dorsal fin is about on a level with the ventrals. The eye is a brilliant red. The body of a roach is not so deep as that of a rudd.

It is one of our most colourful of freshwater fish and thrives better in lakes than it does in streams. On the Broads it is most abundant. Rudd will take maggot and worm but my best sport has always come when using bread-flake or plain bread-paste. My float is always a porcupine quill with three turns of fine lead wire twisted at the base to make it self-cocking, no shot below the float. I vary the hook size and type to suit the bait using a Crystal hook No. 12 or 14 for maggots and No. 10 or 12 Round bend for bread and paste.

EDDIES AND WEEDS

While you occasionally find small rudd in eddies and little streams the bigger fish much prefer quiet places in the vicinity of weeds. They are timid fish and easily scared so one must take advantage of any cover available, but always bear in mind that to be a successful rudd fisherman the terminal tackle should be fine, say two-pounds breaking strain, and you must have a plentiful supply of ground-bait to keep the school together once it has been located.

Like the dace, the rudd gives excellent sport on the artificial fly and nymph and the same patterns that will outwit the former will do service for rudd.

In waters where there are large pike a small rudd is an excellent live bait to use, in that its colouring is more brilliant than roach, dace or gudgeon.

LURING BARBEL

This species is not so widely distributed as those fish already mentioned, waters known to contain them include the Thames, Hampshire Avon, Trent and Yorkshire Ouse. It likes fast, deep streams with gravel bottoms and plenty of weed. It is a specialist's fish and the same tackle used for carp will handle barbel. Like carp and tench it is most active during the summer.

I have caught quite a number of them near weirs on the Thames when spinning minnows and gudgeon for trout, but nothing over six pounds. I have also taken five small ones on artificial flies when fishing for sea trout on the Hampshire Avon, at Winkton Weir. The patterns that lured them were the Butcher and Teal and Black. I believe that they were taken, because under water the

Figure 16. Tackle for barbel.
1. Split shot.
2. Pierced bullet.
3. Split shot.
4. 18 inches between split shot to hook.
5. No. 8 round-bend worm hook.

silver body of the flies may have looked like a small fry of some fish or another.

However, if you want to go after big barbel, the best way I know is to bottom fish, with float or ledger. Baits can range from a nice fat lob-worm, to half-a-dozen maggots or bread-paste. Hooks can be size six to size ten and for worm round bends are best. With ledgering I use a couple of swan shot, or a quarter-inch diameter pierced-bullet, with stops of split dust shot. The largest barbel taken by me, a nine-pounder, was taken on pierced-bullet tackle, see sketch how to make it. Of course in very fast water you may have to use a much heavier weight, but the use of a pierced-bullet enables the fish to pick up the bait without feeling the weight until it has travelled about six or eight inches.

If you are roach fishing in a fast stream and you are broken by a big fish it is "odds on" that the culprit is a barbel so the best thing to do is fix up the proper tackle and go after him.

With float fishing your bait should be no more than two or three-inches off the bottom. Once you have located a barbel haunt, ground-bait with maggots or worms the night before you go fishing. Get to your swim as early in the morning as possible and stay as late as your licence allows, for barbel are most active during dusk, night-time and dawn. While fishing don't forget to throw in a little ground-bait now and then and should you hook a good one take your time and all should be well. Hurry the job and it will end like so many fish stories, broken tackle and the angler bemoaning the loss of a good fish.

Barbel are no good for the table so unless you want to weigh him in for a prize release your catch as carefully as possible, for they are not so tenacious of life as either the carp or tench.

4

Pike tactics and baits

THE gamest freshwater fish of all is without a doubt the
pike. Salmon and sea trout are not freshwater species,
entering rivers only for the purpose of procreating their
kind, and trout are classed as game fish. However, game
though he is very few people like him, he is so greedy,
so tyrannical and savage that nearly everyone's hand is
against him. Maybe Nature is a little to blame for this,
for in fashioning the pike She gave him the general out-
line of a shark and the temperament of a tiger. Nothing
that swims beneath or on the water's surface is safe when
he is on a feeding spree.

All pike are fish eaters, but occasionally one will, like
a tiger, change his feeding habits. The tiger becomes a
maneater and the pike changes to catching voles, rats,
ducklings and water-hens. A friend of mine who for years
was a keeper on the famous Hampshire, River Test, once
told me that when a pike changed to feeding on animals
and water-fowl he kept at it and only took fish when
animals and ducks were not available. My friend once
snared a 20 lb. pike inside which he found five young
mallard ducks and a water-vole.

Young readers may like to know that pike were first
brought to this country by order of Henry VIII, in 1537.
For years they were so valued as food as to cost more
than salmon, game or poultry. Today the pike is of wide
distribution; most rivers and natural lakes have their

quota. But it is no longer valued as a table fish. For my part I like to eat pike providing it has been caught in a river and is not above six pounds in weight. Large pike are coarse eating and those from lakes usually have a muddy flavour.

There are four recognised methods for the catching of pike, live-baiting with float and paternoster tackle, ledgering with dead baits, spinning and plug fishing. The last named is an imported technique from America. Of the four I much prefer spinning with natural or artificial baits and plug fishing. However, there will always be arguments as to which method produces the largest fish, many anglers hold to the belief that a live bait will account for the better fish but it is well to remember that Mr. John Garvin's record 53 lb. pike taken from Lough Conn (Ireland) in 1920, was lured by a $2\frac{1}{2}$ inch, gold and silver spoon and on the same day he caught a 30 pounder with the same bait. The late Alfred Jardine, who held the English pike record for some years with a 37 pounder, caught his fish on a spoon.

Another point in favour of spinning tackle is that the gear is lighter and less bulky; there is no bait can to carry, nor for that matter is it necessary to spend valuable time catching bait. Then again a spinning bait covers a much wider area and therefore it is reasonable to suppose that the angler's offering is seen by more potential customers during a day's fishing than a live bait would be. The wise novice, of course, will give each method a good trial and then and not before will he be able to decide which he prefers.

One trait in the life and habits of a pike stands out as a fault, because it makes him vulnerable to his greatest enemy—Man. This fault is his insatiable curiosity and the angler who remembers this will always get the most sport. Another point to bear in mind is that large pike, say 20 lbs. and over invariably lead a lonely life. Selecting a place with plenty of cover, but always near the feeding places of other fish, he will stay there for months on end, moving out only when the spawning urge compels him to do so.

My rod for live-baiting and spinning is the same—a nine-footer of hollow glass which I also use when spinning for salmon. It is a two-piece with plenty of action and also "back-bone". A rod that is stiff with little or no action has a tendency to pull out the hooks when the angler strikes, whereas a rod with a spring in it will drive in the hooks with the whip developed by striking.

As to the reel the novice should rely on a fixed spool for the reasons I stated in a previous chapter. The reel should be capable of holding 100 yards of 15 lb. breaking strain line, which can be of nylon monofilament or braided nylon. For long distance casting a monofilament line is best with a ball-bearing swivel at the end to which is

Figure 17. Live rudd on snap tackle.
1. How bait is impaled.
2. A snap tackle hook.

fastened an 18-inch, 15 lb. wire trace, with another swivel in the middle. The bait tackle I used for years was that well-known one, the Jardine snap tackle, the two treble hooks of which are fastened direct to the wire in such a

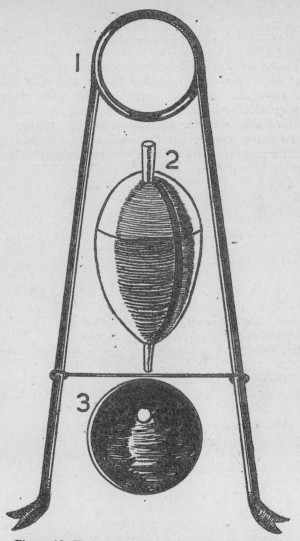

Figure 18. Three items of tackle when pike fishing.

1. Gag to assist in removal of hooks.
2. "Fishing Gazette" float.
3. Pilot float.

way as to have one hook impaling the back of the bait and the other hooked near the bait's head. These hooks are of a special design in that a small hook is what is used to hold the bait (see sketch).

The float is known as a "Fishing Gazette". In shape it is like an egg and has a hole through the middle from which the peg can be withdrawn. There is a slot cut into the side, the line is put into the slot, the peg is replaced and so tightening on the line keeps it in place. A most useful type of float and quite easy to make at home out of cork once you have a pattern (see sketch). In addition to the fixed float some anglers use a pilot float. This is simply a spherical cork of one or two inches in diameter with a hole through the centre through which the line is passed, and is thus free to run up and down the line. When a pike has taken the bait the fixed float will submerge, while the pilot float remains on the surface to indicate the approximate position of the fish as he runs with the bait in his mouth.

Likely places to find a large pike in rivers include, pools without much current, lay-byes, near the mouth of a feeder stream and on the edge of weed beds.

The pike's eyes are near the top of his head so a live bait should not be on the bottom. However, we will assume that the tackle is assembled, the bait a lively six-inch dace has been put on the hooks, a spiral lead is on the line just above the ball-bearing swivel and we are ready to make our first cast.

The place selected is a little channel between the rushes six or seven yards from where we are standing. The bail-arm of the reel is lifted and with a nice easy swing the bait lands a little to the left of the spot selected. The float wobbles, then rights itself and moves slowly back and forth as the bait swims up and down. The dace becomes agitated and the float indicates this by bobbing up and down, then it disappears, we strike almost immediately and the line runs sharply through the rings and you have hooked your first pike. Not a very big one, but let him run around for a few minutes fighting the bend of the rod and the pressure exerted by the reel clutch, which is set not too tight. Bring him in slowly so that I can slip the net under him. There he is ours, about seven pounds, not too bad for your first attempt. You don't want to keep him, O.K. we will remove the hooks and pop him into the water. A pike's teeth are dangerous so we will use the gag to keep his jaws apart and with that pair of small pliers in the bag we will soon have the hooks out. There you are he is safe to handle now, but before you release him note the colouration, a marvellous form of camouflage by Nature, perfectly suited for life among weeds and rushes.

You will have noted our strike was made at almost the same time as line began to leave the reel. There are two schools of thought on the question of what is the right time to strike. One school insists that the angler should not strike until the pike is back in his hiding place, by that time he will have started to swallow the bait, they wait another minute or two and then strike hard. However, it has been my experience that when using snap tackle the strike should be made as soon as possible after the pike starts to run. I have, however, used both methods, the quick strike and the slow one and have lost fish with both, so you must decide for yourself as to which method suits your temperament. One thing is certain of the two methods that of quick striking seems to be more in keeping with ethics of the sport, in that the pike is always hooked in the mouth. With the slower strike there is present the danger of the bait being swallowed, in which case the fish has to be killed so that the hooks can be removed. A single hook is fairly easy to take out with a disgorger, but a treble hook and maybe two in the throat of a fish can prove a messy and difficult job. Frankly I never like to kill fish unless they are to be used as food, hence my main reason for advocating the quick strike.

While we used a dace as our bait it is only fair to say that a gudgeon, roach or rudd might have lured that pike just as well, and whereas we used snap tackle we could have used one treble hook. As previously stated I used snap tackle for years, today I use one treble hook, to impale the bait just behind the dorsal fin or in the top

61

lip. With one hook the bait is more active, striking is just the same as when using snap tackle.

Before leaving the question of live-bait the best wire I have found for making up traces is Alasticum, this can be purchased from most tackle shops. Reason for using wire next to the hook or hooks as the case might be, is that a pike's teeth can sever the strongest nylon. Like many other anglers I have taken fish on nylon traces, but to be on the safe side take my advice and use wire.

PLUGS AND SPINNING BAITS

When pike are lethargic and unwilling to bite it is necessary to tease them a little in order to produce a strike. The characteristic of all pike is to display anger when disturbed during one of their rest periods, and bearing this in mind I rely on the following method to rile up their scales.

Select a plug of the semi-underwater kind of from four to six inches in length, which floats when not in motion and travels about eight to twelve inches under water when reeled slowly. The ones I like are jointed at the middle which gives them a zig-zag motion when being retrieved. There are many colour variations, but the two which have produced best for me are a red head and white body and one that has a green back and yellow underside.

Cast the plug far out over the water near a likely pike haunt and permit it to drop with a splash. Allow the plug to lie motionless a couple of minutes, then, holding the rod downwards, lift it quickly and the plug will dive and then pop back to the surface as the line slackens. Keep the plug bobbing up and down, sometimes reeling it at a rapid pace, causing it to travel fairly deep, then with an abrupt stop permit it to bob upward again and let it lay motionless on the surface, a minute or so and repeat the operation.

Any pike in the vicinity will watch the peculiar antics of the invader for a brief spell and then will apparently get so annoyed that it will dart forward and attempt to crush the life out of the funny looking performer. Then the real battle begins.

It is not my idea, but one that I saw practised in Canada and the U.S.A. more than 40 years ago, always with the same result. For while you may fish different likely spots for an hour or more eventually you will find a pike that will strike and strangely enough it is usually a female that has a go, thus proving, up to a point, that their patience is not so great as the male. On occasions I have seen two pike charge at the same plug.

Practically all plugs can be made to perform new tricks by merely handling the rod and line in ways which are perhaps a little unethical insofar as "good" angling form is concerned. But who cares when by experimenting with something new a fish can be made to strike?

The only hazard I have discovered when teasing pike in this way is that a fish will sometimes strike when the line is too slack for successful setting of the hooks. Therefore it is well not to permit the line to lie coiled or loose upon the water. When the bait has been dropped upon the surface the line should be reeled in carefully so that the bait itself will not be disturbed until you make it dive or perform other tricks. Keep a tight line so that you can drive home the hooks in the event of a fish striking when least expected—and that generally is when they do strike.

Plug fishing is not easy, since a very decided degree of skill is necessary in the successful placing of the plug, probably more so than in casting a wet fly for salmon. I have seen beginners cast a very creditable fly line on the first day out, but it takes considerable time to work a novice plug-caster out of that class. And when it comes to placing a six-inch plug in a two feet pocket between lily-pads some anglers never learn.

Plugs certainly lure strikes, but they also lose plenty of fish. It may be difficult for the uninitiated to realise that a fish can hit a bait armed with two or three treble hooks and miss the hooks, or being hooked, throw the plug; but both are frequently done.

The plug is an American invention and much of the criticism against it comes from anglers who seldom or never have used them. It is a deadly looking bait, but it is not appearances we are considering, rather it is the ability of one bait to produce when others do not.

One thing I have learned in pike fishing is this. All the best haunts will be in those parts of a river or lake that get the most sun. Such spots can be easily detected because the weeds, rushes, etc., will be of better growth than in those parts where there is little sun. Luxuriant underwater vegetation means plenty of food for small fish, thus it provides a well-stocked larder for pike.

Readers may think I am making out a case against live-bait, but that has not been the intention. I am looking at it from the point of view of one who fishes for the pleasure that fishing and fishing problems afford, rather than one who is out to catch fish only.

SPINNING

Artificial baits for spinning come in all shapes and sizes, but if ever restricted to the use of one, my choice would be a spoon. It is the oldest artificial known and the identity of the inventor is shrouded in antiquity, however it is on record that spoons made out of bone and pearl-shell were used in China over a thousand years ago. The two patterns of spoons I always have with me are a silver wobbling spoon and the Colorado, both are pretty deadly when pike are roaming about near their hides.

When spinning always remember that more fish have been lost through speedy manipulation of the reel handle than have ever been caught. Pike are not fools, and a bait that comes whizzing past is more likely to alarm than interest them. On the other hand if the bait is kept moving along at a steady pace it has a better chance of inviting a bite.

If there is a quantity of lead on the trace it is impossible to follow this technique because the bait has to be moved rapidly to prevent it sinking to the bottom.

The silver wobbling spoon has two treble hooks, the Colorado has one, but wound round the shank is some red wool and a lead weight is on the wire that holds the

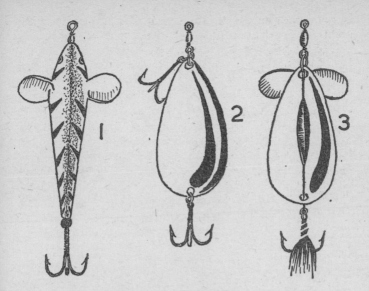

Figure 19. Artificial baits.
1. Brown and Gold Devon minnow.
2. Silver wobbling spoon.
3. Colorado spoon.

hook. It also has spinning vanes and is the ideal bait for long distance casting, in deep and open water.

The next bait I favour is the devon and the two colourations preferred are green and yellow, and brown and gold. Here again the bait should not be worked too fast.

A 15 lb. line is quite heavy enough for most places but on a lake where very large fish are known to be, it might be advisable to increase the line strength to 18 or 20 lb. With all types of spinning one needs to use an anti-kink, in deep water lakes a suitable Wye-lead can be used, but in river work my choice is an anti-kink made of celluloid, with a swivel at one end. The swivel is attached to the trace, the link to the line (see sketches). One can also use dead natural baits such as dace, gudgeon, etc., but special tackle is required.

C

This is another old-time method of pike fishing and is still an easy way of luring a fish in those places where it is impossible to spin. Pike paternosters can be purchased at most tackle dealers and once you have a pattern they are easy to make at home. Live baits I have found to be good are gudgeon and dace but don't have them too big, then even if you do not get a pike you may hook a large perch as they favour similar places to feed. Some anglers get the idea that if they are using a large bait, and I have seen roach and rudd of one pound weight and over used, they are more likely to take a big fish, but it does not work out that way for I have seen several twenty-pounders and three thirty-pound pike taken on three and four-inch baits. Always lip-hook your baits (see sketch) when using a paternoster.

LEDGERING

In recent years a good many large pike, of over 20 lb., have been caught on ledgered baits such as dead roach,

Figure 20. Anti-kinks.
1. Wye lead.
2. Celluloid.

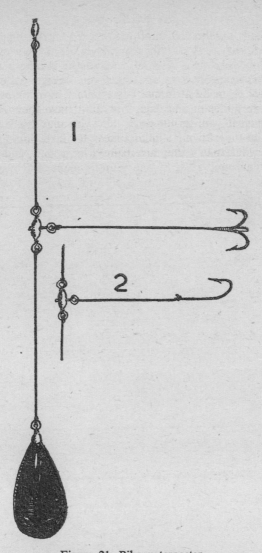

Figure 21. Pike paternoster.
1. Paternoster with treble hook on boom.
2. Boom with single hook.

rudd, herring and sprats, but for ledgering one has to have a good deal of patience. Having done very little of it I do not propose to deal with the subject. I can say the same about trolling on a lake. In both methods very little skill is required in presentation of the bait, of course, if one is tired after a couple of hours spinning here and there, or if one is having a meal it is a good and sometimes profitable way of whiling away the time.

5

Grayling—Silver lady
of winter

ALTHOUGH a member of the Salmonidae tribe the grayling, due to its breeding period, is classed with freshwater species. That in no way alters the fact that it is a game fish. It is not so widely distributed as trout and only a few rivers have them. However, when the countryside is aglow with apples and nuts, grayling fishing comes into its own.

Many thousands of words have been written regarding other members of the Salmon family, but very few about the grayling. There is no doubt that it has gained a bad reputation on preserved trout waters through its alleged partiality to trout spawn. Another trait it is accused of is that of bullying trout and driving them out of suitable feeding places. However, in my opinion the one great fault with this fish lies in the fact that it breeds much faster than trout. But one thing is certain, where there are grayling, you can be sure that the water is pure and well oxygenated, for they will not stay in water that is not.

In the North of England and in many parts of the South, the grayling is known as the "Silver Lady" or "Lady of the stream". Her ladyship is coy, fickle, capricious, flirtatious and gullible, sometimes accepting at the tenth time of asking that very fly or bait which nine times she has declined.

Be that as it may, the grayling is a most convenient and obliging fish—the flyfisher's stop-gap—coming into season as the trout go out, and contrariwise.

Those who have fished for both trout and grayling have observed a marked difference in their way of feeding. Trout if they are in the mood, will often rise at any fly of a tempting colour and reasonable size. Grayling will ordinarily do no such thing, for red and green are the two main colours that intrigue them. Then again while you can take trout on size eight and ten flies in the evening grayling rarely rise to such sizes, so when you try your luck with a fly, with grayling as the quarry keep your flies to No. 14, 16 and 18, with the terminal tackle no more than three pounds breaking strain.

Their haunts vary with the seasons, as also with the temperature of atmosphere and water. In autumn they resort chiefly to sandy and gravelly shallows, loving especially the edge of the current. Later, following a few heavy night frosts, they lurk in placid depths.

However, my young readers know very little about fly fishing yet, so their search for grayling will of course be with float tackle and bait.

Trotting with one or two maggots as bait is an ideal way to capture a brace or two from water that has some movement. The float should be a small egg-type "cocking" when two or three dust shot are nipped on the three pound nylon line three to six inches below the float. The hook on which the maggots are impaled can be No. 14, 16 or 18 depending on the state of the water. If it has colour from recent flooding use the No. 14, if clear or shallow No. 16 or 18 will do, but use eyed hooks so that you can tie them direct onto your line after the float is in position.

Upon the float stopping or commencing to bob strike immediately by simply raising the rod top smartly. It will be found that nine times out of ten the best rises will follow a frosty period. Dace and small chub also like similar water and quite often your bait will be taken by one or the other, but that is all in the fun of the game. You never know what will take when trotting.

Figure 22. Grayling float for worm or maggot.

To give an example of what I mean. Last year a friend of mine Roy Chilvers, well-known Hampshire game and sea-angler was "trotting" for grayling at Fordingbridge, on the Hampshire Avon, when a maggot was taken by a big fish which kept him busy for nearly an hour, before he was able to tail it out. The fish was a salmon kelt of 12 pounds, not a bad feat on a three pound line. That was during December and I happened to be fishing with Roy at the time. We propped the fish up with stones at the side of the stream and in ten minutes it was strong enough to swim away. I hope it got back to the sea safely.

Another bait that has accounted for some fine grayling is a small red worm, which should be allowed to move down the swim about 8 or 10 inches from the stream bed. Keep your worms in a container in which there is plenty of clean moss and have with you a match-box filled with fine sand. Before trying to put the worm on the hook dip it in the sand and it will be much easier to handle. Believe me trying to put a lively worm on a hook in bitter cold weather takes some doing when your fingers are numb. But whether you are using maggot or worm don't let your eyes wander, keep watching the float as it trips along. Grayling bites can be tricky for quite often the float dives under in a flash and when you strike nothing happens. You have to be very clever, indeed, to register every bite. I have been fishing a good many years and have not mastered the art yet.

They move around in small schools so once you have caught one throw in a few small maggots to keep them interested, and you should, with careful fishing, manage to get another one or two. Use your net to land a grayling and don't be in too big a hurry, for in winter, in particular a hooked one fights very hard. Once you have one hooked it is very rarely that they break free. I appreciate accidents can happen, but by and large, once on the hook he is yours. Reason being that a grayling shoots up from the bottom, takes the bait and goes down again, in so doing the hook is driven into leathery lips or the side of the jaws.

If they are not interested in natural baits, maybe an artificial lure will do the trick and the one that is most in evidence on grayling waters is known as a "grass-hopper". I have never been able to understand where it got such a name for it is nothing like the insect after which it is named. It is made by wrapping fine lead wire around the shank of a No. 12 long-shanked hook as a foundation to give it weight; then over the lead is wound green pea-cock herl. The feather from which the green herl is obtained is known as the sword. This produces what I believe grayling mistake for a grub of some kind. The "grass-hopper" is fished sink and draw. In other words you raise your rod top thus lifting the bait and then lower the rod slowly and back down goes the "grasshopper". After a flood, when the fish are congregated in the quiet lay-bys near the banks the "grasshopper" can be very deadly.

About 35 years ago I was on a fishing holiday in Finland, that was before the country was over-run by the Russians. I was in the Petsamajoki region and was having reasonable sport with both trout and grayling when along came a Kolta Lapplander, with a very large sack on his back, this was nearly full of four and five pound trout and grayling. He watched me for a while and then indicated I should try the lure he had used. I don't know its proper name so have simply called it the Finnish Lure, needless to say I had excellent sport in that country with it and on several waters in this country.

Like the "grasshopper" it is very simple to make and here is how to do it: A long-shanked No. 12 hook is given a few turns of fine lead wire to make it sink quickly. Over this is wound some black wool which is then ribbed with yellow wool. At the head is wound a black cock hackle, which is cut very short. On the original given to me the hackle was black deer hair, but I find a black hackle does just as well and is much easier to obtain. Like the "grasshopper" it is fished also, sink and draw.

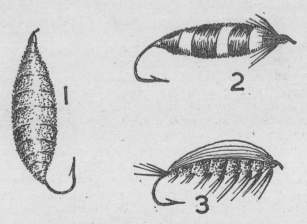

Figure 23. Grayling lures.
1. Grasshopper.
2. Finnish lure.
3. Freshwater shrimp.

73

A third artificial lure on which I have had some of my largest winter grayling is the Shrimp. It is not quite so easy to make as the other two, but with a little practice any boy or girl could create one. Here is how it is made. An ordinary No. 12 fly hook is used and the tail is composed of half-a-dozen fibres from a Rhode Island cock hackle cut short, the body is light brown wool which is ribbed with a small Rhode Island cock hackle cut short. The casing which covers the top from tail to head is made out of a narrow strip from a cock pheasant's tail feather.

A glance at the sketches will give an idea what the finished product should look like. Materials for these lures can be obtained at most tackle shops.

WORM FARM

Before we leave this chapter on grayling a few words on how to obtain worms right through the season. Maggots can be purchased from tackle dealers, but worms are not so easy to come by in winter and the only sure way I know is to farm your own.

Many anglers produce their own supplies by having a wooden box sunk in a shady spot in the garden. The one I use is three feet in length, two-feet, six-inches in width and two feet in depth. Fill the box with damp, rich earth in which there is plenty of leaf-mould. To stock your farm put in about 50 sturdy worms and in about four months time there will be a stock of nice baits sufficient to last one angler a season, fishing two days a week. Remember to put on an adequate cover in times of excess rain or frost.

There is no fear of "fishing" out your worm farm. Worms reproduce rapidly by eggs which are laid in little capsules. The young become adult in about four months, but it is the half-grown ones that are the best baits for grayling. Any time you find sickly looking worms on the soil surface, take them off and throw them away or they will contaminate the rest, they will die and you will have to clean out your farm and start all over again. If you look after it, your worm farm will last some years.

Worms eat earth, that is they pass it through their bodies, extracting the organic matter. A liberal sprinkling of leaf-mould every two or three months will keep them happy.

Two or three days before you intend going fishing take out the number of worms you think you will need and put them in a receptacle (tin) containing nice clean, but damp moss. The worms will clean themselves in this and be very active when needed for the hook. When you return from fishing don't put left-over worms back in the farm, they might have been damaged, rather put them on the garden where they will soon dig themselves in.

Grayling are good table fish, in fact I like them just as much as trout, so with any fish over 10 inches you can be sure of a most tasty meal. Anything under that size should be returned. Of course on some waters like the River Test, all grayling caught, on many stretches no matter what size, have to be killed. A great pity when there are so many little streams in the country that would suit them.

6

Game Fishing
Trout

THE glamour that surrounds salmon, sea trout and trout fishing grows with the passing of the years, and quite naturally more and more teenagers are attracted to it. Many newcomers, I am sorry to say, have a very lean time for the first two or three seasons before experience teaches them what to do.

This trial and error business, however, can be of long duration with some youngsters, so in this section on game fishing we will try to find a few short cuts to success.

Born in North Wales, I was one of those fortunate individuals in that I lived many years within sound of a splendid salmon and sea trout river. Within one hour's walk from my home there were several streams and lakes containing large numbers of trout, a few char and freshwater fish. My parents and grand-parents were keen anglers, so at an early age I was put on the right road. In many respects what I learnt during those formative years still holds good.

One of my first lessons, I think it was shortly after my seventh birthday, was how to read Nature's signposts on a trout stream. Some people never seem to learn that being able to read a stream is just as important as using the right kind of tackle at the right time. They go on year after year in the same old way and wonder why it is they don't have better sport.

In every stream there are good and bad areas and of course those anglers who live near the water know the taking places. A newcomer must find them and if he is able to read a stream his task is made easy in that he fishes those places where he knows fish are likely to be. The old trial and error method with its loss of valuable time is thus, to a large degree, eliminated. Minus that ability the beginner's visit is practically doomed to disappointment at the beginning, and so we hear that timeworn and hackneyed phrase "Oh, they were not biting today."

Let us look at the average trout stream. Trout, must like human beings, eat to live. Granted under certain water temperatures their digestive organs are slowed up, but eat they must.

Trout love oxygen and on every water you will find on investigation places where there are underwater springs, fast streamy stretches ending in pools and feeder streamlets. Wherever oxygen is plentiful there you will find the largest number of trout. Instinct tells them that such a place provides food of one kind and another. If such a place is devoid of adequate cover, then large fish will only feed there in late evening and under cover of darkness.

Trout require cover and by cover is meant rocks, subsurface plant growth, over-grown and under-cut banks, fallen trees and so on. In pools and streamy water that has little cover you will find that whilst the six and seven inchers will feed during the day, the big fellows will wait till late evening before they venture from their hides.

Isolated weed-beds well out from the bank are usually a sign of spring water bubbling up. Such beds are the natural breeding grounds for all kinds of aquatic insects and crustacea on which trout feed.

At times such places are difficult to locate, but once they are found the angler who uses nymphs on his cast will be well repaid for his trouble. In such localities nymphs are a deadly lure throughout the entire season irrespective of weather and water conditions. In Scotland I have seen trout taken on nymphs in a snow blizzard when glycerine had to be used to prevent the line from freezing to the guides, and also in a heat wave during the middle of July with the water crystal clear.

Be on the alert for obstructions that divide a stream such as islands or extra large boulders. Trout, are always attracted to where the separated currents rejoin, for their collision sets up a turbulence that scours a pocket in the bottom and keeps things stirred up in general. The currents work against each other often resulting in a patch of fairly calm water well below the dividing line. I have lured many fine trout from such places by approaching from down-stream and casting wet-flies or nymphs above where the currents converge.

THEY LOVE SHADOWS

Another characteristic of trout is that they love the places where there are plenty of shadows and in the spring with very little over-head cover the best fish will lie close into the bank sides.

During periods of warm weather they are attracted to fast water, but don't look for them directly in spume and froth. The trout will lie just down-stream from the rush of water or at the side of the main flow. Sharp bends are also good fishing places and most of them conform to a fairly standard pattern. A shallow bottom and slow water extends out from the inside bend, whereas the opposite side is marked by a strong current and a fairly deep channel. Trout will feed tight up to the far bank where the current thrusts against the shore and sweeps in insects and other floating food. The near edge of such a current is often marked with a stretch of fairly slack water and it is from such a place that one can often pick up a brace of really good fish.

Occasionally one will come across pools that have everything to interest trout, depth, cover and currents in just the right combination. The water drops in with a frothy tumble, slides down one side of the pool, loses speed, and finally picks up again to scoot smoothly out of the pool. Opposite the main current a big eddy will rotate majestically. Where will the fish be? Everywhere! In the current, in the slack area and in the tail of the run. The only mistake YOU can make is to leave any part of it untried.

However, no matter what type of water you may decide to fish try and refrain from wading and keep well back from the bankside when casting for the ground acts as a sounding-board, which sets up vibrations that travel for yards in the water resulting in the scaring of the fish in that area. A trout may not have a very large brain, but that is no indication that he is a fool, if you think so, just think of the skill, patience and perseverance the most expert of anglers put into the job of luring one or two. The solution is to keep away from the banks and out of the water as much as possible. A pound trout can be reckoned as a good fish in most waters, but he has only reached that size by being wary, and what is more he will in most cases be caught by someone who is a little wiser than himself.

Whenever I see a kingfisher gazing into a pool from an overhanging branch, nine times out of ten it indicates a school of minnows and where these little fish are, there you will find some specimen fish. If bait fishing is allowed, a slowly spun minnow during early morning or late evening will invariably produce a nice trout or two.

Another pointer is that where there is erosion of banks, insects and worms are washed into the stream by the action of the water. Up-stream worm or the impaling of a beetle on a hook is then indicated. Herons love such places and on the River Llugy (Wales) some years ago I watched a heron for half-an-hour during which time he speared five seven inch trout. Nature has equipped this greatest of all anglers with the ability to locate the best spots. A menace on a stream, maybe, but he is also useful in that he often shows an angler where fish are.

Before starting to fish an unfamiliar water spend at least an hour looking the situation over, then map out your campaign, always remembering that the easy to get at places will have been fished many times. The more difficult a place is, the more chance you have of battling with a worth-while trout. From what I have noted over the years a great many anglers are always in too great a hurry to get to the next pool or stream and so miss Nature's signposts. The angler who observes and reads a water looks for them and profits accordingly.

When you go to purchase your tackle have someone with you who understands such things. An eight foot hollow-glass rod would be O.K. for small streams, but if you intend fishing a fairly wide river, also lakes and reservoirs then a nine-footer would be much better. You would, with a little practice, be able to cast farther and control much larger fish. Such a rod could also be used for sea trout fishing.

Actual weights of rods are hard to standardise. The action is the important thing, and here again there is considerable difference of expert opinion. My own description of the proper action for both wet- and dry-fly fishing, which is most easily described in terms of curvature induced by suspension of a two-ounce weight from the tip when held in a normal fishing position, is a gradual and evenly increased curvature from butt to tip. Expressed geometrically, this would be slightly greater curvature than half a parabola or between that and a semi-circle. I have no use for the "tip-action" rods—those with butts stiff as a poker and the second joint nearly as bad with tips that take practically all the flexes of casting. For any, but short casts their action is decidedly jerky and their tips will not stand up to continuous pressure.

I have no doubt you will be told by some people that you will need two fly rods, one for wet-fly and one for dry-fly fishing. From my own experience I have proved to many anglers, time and time again that if one can cast and present a wet-fly properly the same can be done with its dry counterpart with the same rod.

BEST KIND OF LINE

Once you have decided on your rod there is the question of a line. Every reputable rod-maker recommends the size of line that is best for the action and weight of rod and it does not do to go against such advice. However, a floating plastic coated line will be found to serve very well for both types of fly-fishing, but make sure the line is tapered, for such a line aids casting. In the old days we had oil-dressed silk lines and for dry-fly work they had to be dressed with a line floatant; today that is a thing of the past, the modern line will float all day without attention. Another advantage of a floating line is that the rod can lift it off the water without undue strain.

You now have the rod and line, the next item will be backing for the line and for all my lines, salmon included, I use 10 lb. braided nylon which is spliced to the fly line. For trout and sea trout 30 yards is quite sufficient. Some anglers use nylon monofilament as backing, but I have found that braided nylon, being much softer in texture is better.

Be sure to purchase a good reel. There are a number of excellent ones available at moderate prices, but purchase the one that is the lightest in weight. Forget anything you might hear about a reel having to balance the rod. The only function the reel has to perform is to hold the line. If I could get a reel that weighed no more than the weight of a No. 16 dry-fly I would purchase it straight away.

Next we want some leaders. They should be tapered and ranging in length from eight feet to nine feet, but sometimes on a crystal-clear stream I have used a leader of 12 and 14 feet in length. Half-a-dozen of these will do to start off with. Later on you will be able to make up your own from various breaking strains of nylon. For small stream work I like my leaders tapered from six to one pound breaking strain. On waters where big fish are known to exist the taper is increased accordingly and for lake and reservoir work the strength of the leader is much greater having a taper of 10 lb. to 6 lb. This is the same taper I use when night fishing for sea trout and also for grilse fishing (maiden salmon).

THOSE WET- AND DRY-FLIES

Next we want some flies. A volume could be written on

flies alone and many have been. A good wet-fly is sparsely dressed with hen hackles and soft wings, but a really fine dry-fly calls for the acme of perfection in the art of fly-dressing. See that your floating flies have stiff, glossy hackles that stand out perpendicularly from the body, or even slant forward and are evenly spaced around the shank of the hook. Avoid those with soft, lustreless hackles that curl backward and are unevenly wound. Quantity of hackle is sometimes substituted for quality and workmanship, believe me it is a poor substitute. Sparse hackles with good wings will often float better than bulky ones, and they are generally more attractive to fish. To be really effective under most conditions, a dry-fly should ride high on its hackles and tail without relying on its body and wings to keep it from submerging.

Figure 24. Winged wet- and dry-flies and Spider.
1. Winged wet-fly.
2. Winged dry-fly.
3. Spider (hackle) dry-fly.

In both types of flies there are two sorts, classed as hackle and winged. In many instances I have found that hackle flies (spiders) produce better than winged ones and in the case of dry-flies a spider will always float much longer than a winged fly.

Now what flies should we purchase, I know they all look pretty in their show-cases and quite a number have fancy names, as a start we could select two March Browns, two Greenwell Glory's, Wickham's Fancy, Iron Blue Dun, Dark Olive Dun, Pale Olive Dun, Black Spider, Partridge and Yellow Spider, Gold-ribbed Hare's Ear Spider and

Red Tag Spider. This list comprises wet-flies and those other than spiders are winged patterns. All are dressed on size 16 hooks. If you propose doing any evening or night fishing have one or two in size 14. They are all wet-flies, but while we are at it let us select half-a-dozen dry-fly spiders and those I can thoroughly recommend are Greenwell's Glory, March Brown, Iron Blue Dun, Coch-y-Bondhu, Pale Evening Dun and Tup's Indispensable. All are dressed on size 16 hooks with turned-up eyes.

Figure 25. Wet Spider flies and Nymph.
1. Black Spider.
2. March Brown Spider.
3. "Kite's" hook and copper wire nymph.

In addition to wet- and dry-flies we should have three nymphs and the three I use most of all are March Brown, Kite's Imperial and Sawyer's Pheasant Tail.

You will need a box for your flies and there are many to choose from, but get one that will accommodate both wet- and dry-flies. Now we want one of those sprays for annointing the dry-flies to keep them afloat.

We now have our tackle so the next job is to learn a little about the art of casting. If you have a lawn, that is excellent, for after you have grasped the essentials, timing and a little practice will put you on the right road. If you have not got a lawn you can practise in a field or even on the river.

With the reel in position and the line threaded through the rings (guides) we are ready to make our first cast. Pull through the rings enough line so that about 25 feet is lying on the grass straight out in front of you, hold your rod in a horizontal position. Now lift the rod slowly at first then quicken the rise to a sharp snap when the rod is in a vertical position, a momentary pause and the line flies out in a beautiful curve behind you, and as it becomes almost straight you now feel the line tug at the rod, that is the time to start the forward cast. Bring the rod forward smoothly, but quickly, finishing again with a snap of the wrist, and the line travels out in front of you. Stop the rod when it reaches the horizontal position.

Never use any muscles other than those of the forearm and wrist. The keynote of success in casting is that of timing and only practice will bring success. Eventually there will come a time when you will want to make extra long casts, this can be done by "shooting" the line. Here again it is a question of timing. Several feet of line is pulled from the reel and held in loops in the left hand, or vice versa if you are casting left-handed. When the line is driving out in front of you and just before the rod reaches its resting point (horizontal position) the loops are released and the weight of the line still going forward will pull the extra line through the rings.

At no time should you use force; it is the rod that has to develop the propulsion power to start the line going backwards or forward.

Take a short rest now and then while practising and in about two hours you should be able to produce a reasonable cast of 45 feet, which is good enough to take trout on most small streams.

Once you can cast this distance with the line we will attach a leader. For this we want a loop on the end of the line and one on the leader. Take half-an-inch of the plastic skin off the line and tease out the threads, rub them with fly-dresser's wax, and work the threads between finger and thumb until they adhere to the line thus forming a neat loop. Whip the threads to the line with black fly-tying silk as tight as the silk will bear, finishing off with a couple of coats of fly-tying varnish (see sketches 1 and 2). In our third sketch a loop has been tied in the leader and the end of the leader has been put through the line loop. When line and leader are pulled tight you have a strong and very neat connection.

In drawing No. 4 we have the start of a Turle Knot, which I consider to be one of the best for fastening a fly to leader, as it makes a straight connection between the hook shank and leader.

Begin by passing the end of the leader through the hook eye from the front, then slide the fly up the leader out of the way. Make a slip-knot in the end of the leader by bringing the free end around twice, like a double overhand knot.

Draw the knot tight and pass the loop over the fly as shown in sketch No. 5. Pull the leader and manipulate

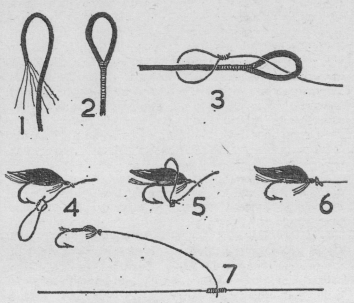

Figure 26. Line loop and knots.

1. Threads in line are teased out.
2. Threads are whipped making a permanent loop.
3. Loop tied in nylon leader, end of leader put through line loop.
4. Start of turle knot.
5. Second stage.
6. Turle knot in position.
7. Nymph as dropper on leader.

85

the loop so that it tightens around the back of the hook eye, and not in the eye or on the leader itself (see sketch No. 6).

In illustration No. 7 we have the Blood knot, which is used for making up tapered leaders and droppers for flies.

To make the blood knot take two pieces of nylon which we will call A and B. Twist the end of B three times around that of A, then pass B through the space formed where the ends just cross. Next twist the end of A three times around B, then pass A in the opposite direction to B through the space formed where the ends just cross. Pull knot tight and cut off ends A and B, unless you want to attach a dropper, in which case you leave one end long as in our sketch which has a nymph attached. If you study the sketches in how to make the Double Three-fold Blood Knot you should have no difficulty in doing it. However,

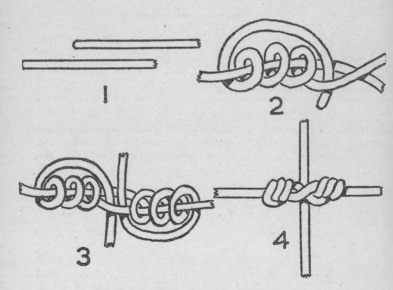

Figure 27. Double three-fold blood knot.
1. First stage of blood knot.
2. Half the knot is complete.
3. Second half is done.
4. Finished blood knot is pulled tight.

before you use nylon it might be as well to put in a little practice with two pieces of string.

Tomorrow we will try to catch a trout, have your tackle ready and I will pick you up in the morning.

ON THE RIVER

Well here we are at the river, now where should a trout be lying in the stretch of water we are looking at? All right, if you think he is there, take a good look at the current to make sure where to place your flies, which I notice are March Brown at point and Greenwell's Glory as the dropper. A good choice and your decision was right to use wet-flies as we have little colour in the water. Now, where is that trout watching for his next mouthful to come from, and where and how will it come to him? Well, that little run near the large boulder seems the most likely place. However, move down a few yards to allow room for the back cast, or you will be up in that tree. O.K. All set? Let's cast. Not bad, but you want to be out another couple of yards. There, that's much better.

"That studying of the water took a lot of valuable time," someone will tell you. Sure it did, but you caught your fish in four casts. With streams as crowded as they are these days, you have to make a little fishing go a long way. The best way to do this is to study the water and all its possibilities, make it yield as much fun and as many fish as you can, even if you put them back again. Fish slowly, thoughtfully, and carefully and you will learn more about trout and their habits than you ever thought possible. Always bear in mind that impatience and muscle are two things that must be avoided if you want to be a good fly fisherman.

One of the main reasons why some anglers do not catch many trout is that they can't get it into their heads that trout are easily scared. They're extremely sensitive to tiny vibrations of the ground caused by a man walking, or knocking pebbles together on the bottom as he wades. And some people seem to think trout can't see very well. Remember that if you can see him, he can see you—

indeed, he probably saw you before you could him and got out of there pretty quick and in so doing alerted other trout in the immediate area leaving the water barren for some time.

A CLOSER LOOK

Before we pass on to the question of dry-flies we will take a closer look at wet-flies including nymphs. We know that the wet-fly has been in use for hundreds of years, the nymph for about 70 years.

For many anglers, fishing sunken flies simply means casting up and across, letting the stream carry the flies where it will, but good trout are rarely fooled into thinking they are food. To be successful the angler must impart "life" to his flies by manipulation of his rod and line. Lifting the rod-tip slightly every now and then as the flies work along the current will result in the hackles (legs) of the flies working back and forth and the wings will open and shut. By pulling on the line, or gathering it in the hand preparatory to making another cast, the flies move quickly through the water as if they were insects of some sort trying to escape. By gathering the line slowly in the hand the flies move up-and-down in little jerks.

MY FAVOURITES

Now while I use several winged patterns my favourite wet-flies are Spiders. In the water such a pattern suggests food while out of it the appearance may suggest a chimney-sweep's brush! However, when submerged, a properly dressed spider changes form. The feather filaments fold back to the body and take the shape of an insect struggling to the surface, or that of a drowned insect. If the spider has a sparsely made fur body it becomes translucent and even more suggestive of food than if it had a tinsel body.

The Black Spider, with its brown fur body and starling hackle, is a good example of this, as is the March Brown Spider with a hare's ear fur body, both these patterns score right through the season because they suggest food and, in colouration represent many kinds of insects.

A friend of mine who has been trout fishing for nearly 70 years uses only two flies all the season through and they are the pair mentioned above. If I were ever restricted to the use of one type of wet-fly my choice would be spiders in sizes No. 14 and No. 16.

In the main the general colouration of most water-borne insects is combinations and tints of black, grey, brown and olive and many are similar in size, so when purchasing flies such colours must be kept in mind.

As with wet-flies so it is with nymphs the keynote being suggestion. One of the most successful nymphs in my box is Kite's Imperial, which was invented by the late Major Oliver Kite, well known for years as a master angler and television personality. "Ollie" as he was always known was a fishing friend of mine and being born in Wales we had a lot in common, in fact his nymph was developed on the River Usk. His nymph has no counterpart in Nature, but it scores because it represents many kinds of nymphs. Another nymph with which "Ollie" used to demonstrate in regard to suggestion of trout food and with which he regularly caught four and five pound trout was composed simply of a No. 16 hook, with fine copper wire wound near the eye to represent the wing-cases of a nymph (see figure 25).

NO MYSTERY

Many writers have made nymph fishing appear considerably more complicated than it really is. Nymphs when they feel the urge to change into the fly proper rise from the river bed to the surface where they hatch out. However, before they get to the surface they will travel many yards down-stream, rising a few inches and falling back. Eventually they reach the surface where they float, the wing-cases burst open, but half-an-hour or even an hour might elapse before the now winged insect is able to fly off. The angler has to represent these movements by manipulation of rod and line.

After a heavy rainstorm fishing the nymph is usually

at its best. One reason why this is so is because the heavier flow of water dislodges nymphs from their holds on rocks, weeds and debris in the stream. They drift down-stream in large numbers.

In striking, rely on speed and not strength. Control the natural tendency to jerk the rod upward in the plane in which your forearm moves when casting. Instead, cultivate a wrist movement that will at once impart motion to the line and so drive the hook point in over the barb.

The nymph has accounted for some very big trout on lakes and reservoirs and I have no doubt will continue to do so because nymphs form more than 90 per cent of a trout's food, whether in stream or lake.

ON LAKES AND RESERVOIRS

On lakes, which includes reservoirs, nymphs for the angler are dressed on hooks a little larger than one would use on a stream. A friend of mine who fishes Blagdon and Chew reservoirs near Bristol at least a dozen times during a season dresses his nymphs on No. 10 and No. 12 hooks. Another friend who fishes the lime-stone lakes in Southern Ireland also uses similar sizes and his largest fish to date is a nine-pounder.

With lake fishing one has to be able to cast a fairly long line, so, until you can manage this, my advice is to stick to stream fishing for at least a season.

Many lake anglers in order to get distance attach 15 to 20 feet of heavy fly line to a backing composed of nylon monofilament. Several yards of nylon are pulled from the reel and left in coils on the ground, or in a line raft, thus when the heavy fly line shoots forward it pulls through the rings, with comparative ease, the 10 or 12 lb. breaking strain nylon. One can cast prodigious distances with this method, but it takes a little practice. However, my advice to all teenagers is, perfect your casting and the "shooting" of your line before starting out on something else, for it is much better to be skilled in one method than be semi-skilled in two or three.

There are some important details about dry-flies for trout which every young fly-fisherman should know if he is to make a wise selection for his individual use. Intelligent application of the points discussed here should make it easy for an angler to know what kind of flies he needs and to make his purchases accordingly.

The first point to consider in selecting dry-flies is to be sure their construction follows established fundamentals whose value has been proved by years of experience. For example the hooks they are dressed on should be made of fine, light-weight wire with up-turned eyes. The reason is that a dry-fly as its name suggests is meant to be fished on the surface, and, if the hooks are heavy, the flies are likely to be poor floaters. Up to a point, the tendency of a heavy wire hook to sink may be off-set by a generous use of stiff hackles, but such an arrangement merely gets the best out of what is a bad situation to start with. The best dry-flies are sparsely dressed on light-weight hooks.

Let's prove this point. A careful inspection of a natural insect will show us that we cannot readily make an exact imitation. Instead we have to be satisfied with a suitable likeness obtained from a combination of feathers, tinsel, fur and what not, dressed on a hook. We cannot construct artificials with hackles so sparse that they simulate the legs of a natural. If we did our imitation would not float. So we must put on enough hackle to support the hook on the surface skin of the water, and the lighter the weight of the hook, the less hackle is needed.

Even with such flies as spiders a sparse dressing is a decided advantage. However, no matter what type of fly, it requires, as I said earlier on, stiff cock hackles, and when purchasing first-quality flies you have a right to inspect them. You can tell them by their glossy sheen and the stiffness of the fibres. Each fibre will stand out by itself and won't merge with the rest. If the hackle is soft, it will look matted and dense near the hook shank, and the ends are likely to curl, especially if they support the weight of the hook for some time. But don't expect to find these quality features in medium or low-priced flies.

Quill-bodied flies are the best floaters of all and many natural flies have the ribbed body which the quill imitates so well.

HAIR WING FLIES

During the last few years a new type of dry-fly has appeared; it was invented in America and has hair wings, hair body and stiff hackle as legs. Lee Wullf is the inventor and on the River Test, his Grey, White and Red Wullf's have killed scores of large trout. The hair used is mainly squirrel and deer and the flies are dressed on long-shanked hooks for the Mayfly season and on ordinary size hooks for general fishing. They are excellent patterns for late evening fishing when larger flies and moths are on the water.

The dry-fly comes into its own when there is a "hatch" of flies on the water. Occasionally you will be at the river and will not see a fly, in a few moments the first flies make their appearance and in a very short time the air is alive with them. The trout know what is happening and in a very short time you will hear plop, after plop as a trout pops his nose up to take a fly.

Your leader should be tapered to two pounds and sprayed with your floatant to keep it on the surface. Select a fly that matches in general size and colouring the natural flies on which the trout are feeding, but make your cast more up-stream than across so that your fly can float down like a natural. Keep your eye on your fly all the time and when you get a rise, strike the same way as if you were using a nymph. If there are big fish moving about increase the size of your leader's taper. When the current starts to drag at the fly as it gets below you, then is the time to make another cast.

Large brown trout are notoriously poor takers during the hours of daylight, but late evening finds them cruising about near the surface feeding hard under the cover of fading light on newly hatched insects, nymphs and spent flies (ones that have laid their eggs and are dead or dying).

An evening rise on lake or stream is a sight worth travelling some miles to see. On such an occasion large areas of water seem to boil so numerous are the fish breaking the surface. However, despite such visible signs, I have frequently heard of an evening rise producing few fish and the question arises, why?

My years of observation have taught me that the drama of the evening rise is divided into four acts and the angler who is aware of this is the one who will profit most.

Very often one hears of anglers forecasting the time of the rise, basing it on what happened the previous evening. On such occasions it is always wise to remember that fishing is not a science, for its methods are not exact, and will not inevitably lead to uniform results. We are dealing with living creatures which have whimsies and feeding habits of their own.

During the summer as the heat goes off the water the wise angler will put up a cast of two nymphs which he will allow to work near the bottom. About an hour of this and a change is made, he works his nymphs just below the surface.

Reason for this is that as the water cools the nymphs that have been most active near the bed of the stream or lake now start to move upwards to the surface.

Now while all this has been going on, trout have not been idle, as some anglers seem to think, they have been busy feeding on the fat, luscious nymphs moving up with them to the surface, hence the need for deep-working and near surface nymphs.

Two acts of the drama have taken place, the third opens with myriads of spent flies dropping on to the water. They are, for the most part, insects that were hatched out 24 hours earlier. In those few hours they have mated, laid their eggs and those that are still alive are floating helplessly in the current or being carried along with the breeze, until their wings become water-logged and they sink below the surface.

For this act the angler puts up a cast of two wet-flies

similar in size and colouration as the ones on the water. Two hours with the wet-fly and the shadows have begun to lengthen. There is still about 90 minutes of daylight left and for this last act the dry-fly angler comes into his own.

Briefly that is the four-act drama of the much-lauded evening rise, a drama that is enacted year after year on streams and lakes wherever there are trout. The angler who comes in at the second or third acts has missed some good fishing and will continue to do so unless he changes his ideas.

OTHER METHODS OF TAKING TROUT

During every trout season there are times when no matter what type of fly, and that includes nymphs, the angler might try the fish are just not interested. For instance the nine weeks period of July and August is usually one of the worst from the stream fisher's point of view—a period when the streams more often than not are low and clear and water temperatures high, with the trout moody as a result. But it does not follow that fish stop feeding; far from it. The wise angler when faced with such a problem leaves his fly-boxes in his pocket and relies on natural insects and bait to lure a few speckled beauties.

Now what are the best "naturals" to use? Craneflies (daddy-longlegs) are good and so are caterpillars, grasshoppers, beetles and blue-bottle flies. In fact any sort of insect that will kick up a fuss when cast on to the water is likely to catch the best trout in the stretch.

However, the best natural bait is our old friend the worm. Like almost every other individual who ever caught a trout as a boy, I started by fishing my bait down-stream. This is the simplest and most easy way to fish. But nowadays I fish my worm up-stream, and can consistently take more fish during poor periods.

Up-stream worming goes back a long way. The technique was probably first developed in Scotland where streams have plenty of movement and are ideal for this particular type of worm fishing.

Using stream currents calls for casts with fly-rod tackle quartering up-stream so that the worm can be forced down into the water by the current. Of course this is impossible to any degree if one uses a tight line. Trout are found in shady places where the water is cool and where they are out of the way of the full force of the current. If a worm is cast well above a trout's hiding place the current will sweep it well down into the water unless the drag caused by a tight line prevents it. If the currents are used to the best ability of the angler the worm will drift naturally just as any other stream-borne bit of food would be. Only in the strongest currents should one resort to a lead weight (split-shot) to counteract the pull, if you can manage without a weight so much the better.

As to impaling a worm, Pennell tackle (two hooks) is best providing the hooks are small, I use No. 16 fly hooks.

Figure 28. Worm on Pennell tackle.

Being small they do not injure the bait so much as large hooks would, and such tackle is easy to make at home once you have a pattern.

A two yard leader is the ideal length and the best method of casting is under-hand, with a little practice it is fairly easy to reach a distance of 35 to 45 feet, which is all you will need on most waters. Accuracy means more than distance. As the bait comes down-stream pull in line and hold the coils in the left hand ready for your next cast. What really takes a lot of practice in up-stream worming is setting the hook on a strike. The instant the bait stops moving with the current, the rod-tip should be lifted to take up any slack. This tightening of the line, will, if a trout has taken the worm, drive home the hooks. With Pennell tackle trout are invariably hooked in the lip, this means that small fish can be returned to the water unharmed.

Natural co-ordination of mind and body is the whole secret, but with practice, a person with only average co-ordination will gradually build up an automatic reflex that will greatly assist in hooking a trout. When you become too tired to maintain complete alertness, it is time to rest. Smart fishermen know when to fish and when to rest.

MORE NATURAL BAITS

Other baits that, at times, can be exceedingly good inclule caddis grub, freshwater shrimp and minnow.

The caddis grub, usually half-an-inch to one inch in length is the larvæ of the caddis fly. The grub is a marvellous architect, it fashions out of bits of wood and grains of sand a home in the shape of a tube to protect it from other creatures. The bits and pieces are held together with a powerful sort of glue it exudes from its body. Sometimes these grub-holding tubes are fastened to the undersides of submerged rocks and debris, but very often the grubs are mobile moving along on their legs from place to place carrying their home with them.

Taking the head of the grub between thumb and fore-finger it is an easy matter to draw the creature from its case. Impale the grub in a rear segment of the body on a No. 16 hook. It can be fished the same as the up-stream worm or used in conjunction with a float. It is a very killing bait during April, May and June. When you have collected a supply leave them in their cases and put in a tin or similar receptacle half-filled with damp moss. Punch a few holes in the lid and the grubs will keep alive three or four days, but you must keep the moss damp.

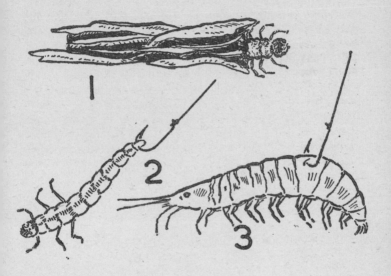

Figure 29. Natural baits.
1. Caddis grub in case.
2. Right way to hook grub.
3. Freshwater shrimp.

The freshwater shrimp is also found under submerged rocks, mostly in gravelly streams. In size it ranges from half-an-inch to three-quarters-of-an-inch. Here again a No. 16 hook is best.

Occasionally in your wanderings you will notice a good trout rising in a place, where it is impossible to cast a fly. When you encounter such a situation collect some caddis grubs or shrimps and with a little time and patience it is quite possible you will catch him. If your grubs or shrimps are on the small side use two or even three on a hook.

Our last natural bait, the minnow, can be fished alive by impaling it through the upper lip, or in the muscle directly behind the dorsal fin. A No. 14 hook will do for very small baits but if they are fairy large use a No. 12 or even a No. 10.

It can also be fished as a dead bait on spinning tackle; such tackles can be purchased from most dealers and like a number of other items once you have a pattern are fairly easy to make. However, before you can do much spinning you will need a spinning rod, but see that it is strong enough for sea trout as well as trout. The one I use for both species of fish is eight feet in length, hollow-glass, two-joint with screw-in reel fittings, and was made from a rod-kit which most tackle-shops stock.

Artificial spinning baits for trout include, spoons, quill minnows and devons of metal, plastic or wood.

7

Game Fishing
Sea Trout

WITH the exception of salmon no game fish is more highly thought of than the sea trout. I caught my first when a schoolboy of 10 years of age and even now, 59 years later, the sea trout still fascinates me.

I have caught these, what I often call "under-studies" for salmon throughout Great Britain and Ireland, Norway and Finland, and although my total score of fish caught must run into many thousand, not once have I been disappointed in the fight each and everyone put up before my net ended the battle.

A most obliging fish it can be taken on natural bait such as worms, maggots and minnows as well as artificial flies, spoons and spinners, so what more could any teenager ask? The knowledge and experience gained when after freshwater fish with float tackle will prove most valuable when one decides to go after these ocean-loving trout. Of course your worm farm will prove invaluable, for sea trout love worms when they are in brackish water and these can be used with float tackle or as bait for ledgering.

Then again the experience you have gained when flyfishing and spinning for trout will stand you in good stead.

A personal friend of mine for many years, the late Sydney R. Dwight, who resided in Berkhamsted, Hertfordshire, and who caught the 22½ lb. record sea trout from the River Frome, Dorset in 1946, always held the view that sea trout were much better fighters than salmon. In many respects I must agree with him for I have yet to battle with one that sulked. In salmon sulkiness is a well-known characteristic.

For the table sea trout from one pound to six pound are the equal of salmon in flavour. However, it has been my experience that fish approaching or in the double-figure class are coarse eating and with very little flavour.

Another thing I have found is that the sea trout once it reaches freshwater loses condition much quicker than a salmon.

As to encompassing their defeat it is a well-known fact that sea trout move in and out of estuaries with the tides, and eventually large schools gather awaiting the right temperature before making the run into freshwater.

Those of you who can get to an estuary frequented by sea trout can expect reasonable sport during April, May and June. The last named two months also marks the move of large schools from the estuaries into the rivers, but as one school moves out another takes its place and this moving in and out carries on until October. An estuary right through the game fish season will always contain its quota of sea trout.

In the early part of a season spinning baits, both natural and artificial will take their toll of the silvery warriors but as the water warms fly-fishing after dark will be found to be the best method to adopt. However, take my advice never go alone, always have an adult with you for his advice and assistance will most certainly be needed should you hook a five- or six-pounder.

In a river that has been coloured by flood-water a large worm impaled on a No. 8, round bend hook is a splendid bait. It should be allowed to roll along the bed of the stream minus a lead weight, the angler releasing a few yards of line at a time. I have had sea trout strike when there has been fifty yards of line out and then the fun really starts when one has to play the fighting fish back to a suitable landing place without disturbing the water too much.

100

Likewise a bunch of maggots, usually five or six, will also prove most attractive in similar water conditions, but use this bait with a float and have the maggots moving along about nine inches to a foot off the bottom. In mid-July and right through August and September when streams are at summer level maggots can prove most

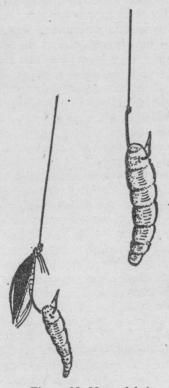

Figure 30. Natural baits.
1. Maggot impaled on fly.
2. Wasp grub on No. 10 hook.

valuable during day-time, when the fish are unresponsive to other offerings from the angler. A maggot on a fly is often excellent and a wasp grub can be good at times.

On the Hampshire Avon, there is a famous sea trout

pool called the Bridge Pool and I have seen as many as 30 sea trout taken in a day by an angler using float and maggots. Fortunately most of the fish were returned. I only mention this to illustrate what a good float angler can do with maggots as bait.

In the previous chapter on trout we dealt at great length with bait, spinning and fly-fishing and as the methods to be adopted are fairly similar when sea trout are being sought I do not propose to repeat them. However there is one phase of fly-fishing that must be dealt with a little more fully, it is using the fly at night.

On more than one occasion people have asked me if I did not think it was a ruinous practice and that by night fishing there would be a gigantic gap made in the ranks of the sea trout family; therefore should the practice of night fishing not be out-lawed? On each and every occasion I have answered that if you could prove to the rank and file fishermen that you could get half-a-dozen every time you went out, they would be "tickled pink" to read about it, but as for going out themselves, thank you so much, they would rather stay at home of an evening and talk about fishing. Mind you there are many who know the worth of night fishing, but it is my contention that it will never become really popular because it occurs during a time when one is given to resting. The inner rebellion to this type of fishing is, in some almost equal to aversion. However, a closer examination of the matter to hand is not out of place and may even wrench even one adult angler out of the depths of his easy chair to accompany a teenager streamward.

In the first place the sea trout is a night-rover and has "eyes for the dark" like the wise old owl and is an inveterate night feeder, and a great lover of pure and well oxygenated water. During the hours of daylight sea trout usually lie in streamy water at the tail-ends of the pools. As dusk merges into night they start feeding and woe betide any minnow, moth or night insect that comes within their reach. They'll hit an artificial fly just as it touches the water and they'll connect just as frequently with a fast moving one. Indeed after a lifetime of fishing for them I would go so far as to say that a fly kept on the move, is more likely to attract than one that is moving at current speed.

Fishing at night is just like fishing in the daytime except that you handle your tackle by touch alone, therefore one should be well acquainted with the water and banks. Good casting and fish-landing places should be memorised. An electric torch is a necessity, but don't wave it round any more than you have to. If you connect with even a three-pounder your work will be cut out for you before he is in the net, that is why a young person should always be accompanied by an adult.

Take the most productive water, water that you know will contain a goodly number of fish. Then fish it thoroughly. Your training while freshwater fishing will now prove its worth, because you will have to exercise the utmost patience and move at a snail's pace.

Now what about flies and tackle. Changes in flies have been taking place over the last few years. When I first started fishing we used ordinary flies for daytime as well as night fishing, then someone realised that sea trout like minnows and fry of other species as a regular diet so flies were created to imitate them. Today we have dozens of colourful lures, demons and terrors. However, while I have caught a good many sea trout on such creations, my best takes during the last few years have been on streamer flies.

Lures, demons and terrors comprise two or more hooks linked together with nylon. The streamer was invented in America at the turn of the century by a well-known Maine angler Herbie Welch, but although he invented more than a score of patterns none has achieved the world-wide success his Black Ghost has. A close second in popularity is the Grey Ghost, but this pattern, more complicated in design was invented by a woman Carrie Stevens of Maddison, Maine. These are two streamers I am never without whenever I go out after dark.

A streamer is dressed on a long-shanked hook and it can be a No. 8 for large fish or No. 10 or 12 for smaller sea trout. When in the water it looks like a minnow or other small fish and if you work it right it acts like one. Make your cast in the normal way, up and across the stream, then when the fly is at the end of its run bring it back in little jerks, this will make the streamer move up and down in the water as if it was a little fish in trouble. Last season I took quite a number of fish by letting the fly wave about in a fast current. If there are any salmon about don't be at all surprised if you hook one when operating a streamer in a current.

Another fly, which also imitates a small fish is the Buck-tail; it is an American invention as well, but is not quite so productive as the streamer. The one I use most is the Black Buck-tail which has a silver tinsel body.

In regard to ordinary flies the patterns I rely on are first and foremost Mallard and Claret, Teal and Black, Peter Ross, Zulu, Black Ghost (streamer), Black Buck-tail and Mallard, Blue and Silver Lure (see illustration).

In giving a list of patterns I appreciate, only too well, that every angler has his own particular ideas, but the above flies have always served me well and newcomers to sea trouting could not do better than start off with them.

DRY-FLIES

Occasionally during a season there are times when sea trout may be rising all over the place, but refuse to have anything to do with the wet-fly, which of course includes streamers and lures; when that time arrives one has to experiment.

Some years ago on the Coquet (Northumberland) I hit such a period and decided to give the dry-fly a try. Of course the hooks used were a little larger, but the same

Figure 31. Sea trout flies.
1. Mallard and Claret.
2. Teal and Black.
3. Peter Ross.
4. Zulu.
5. Black Ghost streamer fly.
6. Black Bucktail.
7. Mallard, Blue and Silver lure.

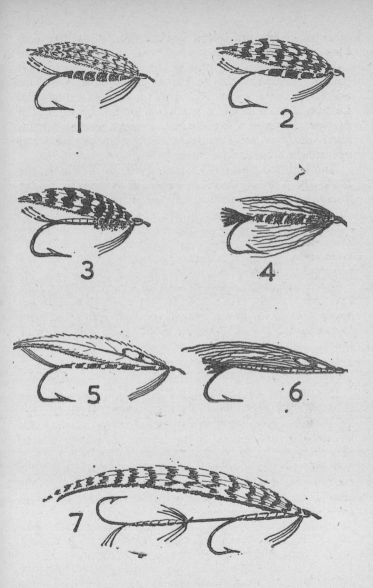

cardinal rules applied in relation to them. They were light in the wire with up-turned eyes, but instead of being dressed with feathers I used deer hair which floats much longer than even the stiffest of feathers.

A scientist friend of mine first suggested deer hair to me as a fly material because of its floatability. This was due, he said, to the fact that most deer hair was hollow, which means that when you make a fly with such material you build in a float as it were. I have taken quite a few sea trout on dry-flies since then, but claim no credit for using such material as the Americans have been using dry-flies made out of deer hair for years. In Scotland there is a famous salmon-fly The Garry Dog or Yellow Garry which is made out of hair.

On the Hampshire River Test most of the dry-flies now in use are made out of hair. On one stretch of this famous river I was asked by the head keeper Mr. Reg Dade to invent a yellow hair Mayfly, this I did and last season many large trout were killed on it.

But to return to sea trout: dry-flies can also prove quite useful when used in mid-light as it were, in other words that short period when the light is fading rapidly to give way to darkness before the stars emerge. Moths and large night flying insects flit across the surface of the water in profusion and the cruising sea trout get quite excited. A nicely placed hair-wing fly will often lure one or two before the rest of the school becomes alarmed and moves off elsewhere.

In the chapter on fly-dressing I will explain how to dress such a fly.

We have dealt with baits, artificials and flies. Now what about rod, reel, line and other equipment. In the first place if you have followed my advice you have no need to bother about your spinning tackle, so we are left with the question of fly-fishing. Straightaway you will need to build yourself another rod and it should have a little more back-bone, than the one you built for trout. It should be of hollow-glass and not less than nine feet in length, if you are in the 16 years to 18 years class then you should be able to handle a 9½ feet rod without any trouble. Such a rod will give you greater casting distance and will enable you to defeat, more quickly, larger fish.

Your reel-fittings should be of the screw-in type and line rings, if you propose to fish an estuary, must be of stainless steel to withstand the corrosion effects of brackish water. Your line should be double-tapered, 30 yards in length and this should be spliced to 50 yards of 10 lb. braided nylon. The tackle dealer will tell you what size line you will require to bring out the spring (flex) in the rod. With too light a line you will not be able to cast very well and a line that is too heavy will strain severely the rod when casting.

A point to remember is that you will always get better service from a tackle shop if the person behind the counter is an angler himself. Any advice he gives you will be sound and based on his own experience. Far too often teenagers are persuaded by non-angling shop assistants to purchase tackle which is useless for the job the purchaser had in mind.

If the net you use for freshwater and trout fishing has a wide mouth it will do for sea trout, but take my advice and paint the handle a brilliant white, then if you should put it down when night fishing it is much more easily located with the aid of your electric torch. While you have the paint handy put a coat on your fly and spinning tackle boxes, believe me if you should unknowingly drop one or the other in long grass, without the assistance of white paint you will have a job finding them. I know because it happened to me one night when fishing the River Tavy (Devon). Fortunately a farmer friend found it and as it had my name inside he knew the owner and came to my hotel the next day to return it.

Before we move on to the next chapter there are a few more things to remember if you want to enjoy your nights out. First never use more than one fly. In daylight it is an easy matter to handle two or even three wet-flies on your leader, but in the dark more than one fly is just asking for trouble, and tangles will occur. Check your fly at intervals to see it is all right. On several occasions I have lost fish through omitting to do this little chore. Occasionally the fly catches in rocks or other obstacles and the hook point is dulled or the barb bent in, and when this happens it is an easy matter for the fish to "throw" the hook.

One of the major problems to personal comfort is the "winged menace". Mosquitoes and other types of blood-suckers can make one's fishing exploits miserable, but there are quite a number of good insect-repellents on the market these days, so before starting out see that you have a tube of repellent in your pocket. Then, when you have got your tackle fixed up at the waterside, anoint your wrists, back of hands, neck and face.

Another thing to carry is a change of socks, for if you have any wading to do it is quite possible that water will go over the top of your thigh boots. It has happened to me on more than one occasion, and fishing in wet feet is unpleasant, to say the least, and can often lead to a nasty cold.

In conclusion, always remember to have a good battery in your torch and to carry a spare bulb just in case you drop the torch and fracture the bulb filament. Years ago I had such an accident and believe me it was not a pleasant experience of having to walk nearly a couple of miles over difficult ground to my car. Ever since then I have carried a spare bulb.

8
Game Fishing
Salmon

WHENEVER I sit down to write about salmon my thoughts go back over the years to the many thrilling battles I had with this, as some people call it, "King of game fish".

I caught my first salmon, a twelve-pounder, about 60 years ago, although it would be more truthful to say the fish caught me. A schoolboy home for the spring term and hoping to catch a trout, I was floating a worm down a beautiful pool on the River Llugwy (North Wales) when the salmon struck. Reason for my fishing the worm was the fact that rain in the mountains had so coloured the water that it was practically useless to use a fly.

When that salmon took hold the shock to my nervous system was such that my hands "froze" to the rod and reel and before I could regain any semblance of mental poise that fish had me in the pool with it.

Fortunately another angler nearby saw my plight, jumped in and helped me out of the pool, the water of which reached to my shoulders. It was also fortunate that my home was nearby so the pair of us were able to get dried out. That fish took my rescuer and I, 20 minutes to subdue.

From that day I have always respected the strength and fighting ability of Salmo Salar.

Not long after this hair-raising experience my parents

109

presented me with my first salmon fly-rod, and I took the fish referred to elsewhere, on a Blue Charm.

IS IT A CLEAN FISH?

Before ever my parents taught me how to fish for salmon I was given several "lectures" on how to tell a clean fish. In the opening months of a season and also in the autumn difficulties may arise in the differentiating between a clean fish and an unclean one. An "unclean fish" is defined by the Act to mean: —

1. Any fish which is about to spawn, or
2. Any fish which has recently spawned and not recovered from spawning.

The onus for correct decision rests with the angler concerned in every case, and the following characteristics by which unclean fish may generally be recognised are as follows: —

From the start of a season to early April most pools will hold fish that have spawned (kelts). In shape they are emaciated, weight disproportionate to length with distension or inflammation of the vent. The fins are usually ragged as is also the tail. The general colouration is dark and dirty, but on occasions especially with an early spawned fish it may be silvery when other indications should be sought. The gills are a dirty pink instead of red and there are nearly always maggots present at the tips, whereas those of a clean fish are nearly always free from maggots.

In contrast to a fish from the sea, a kelt's mouth is full of sharp teeth.

Fish about to spawn (latter part of a season) are very swollen along the flanks and belly. Slight pressure on flanks may cause emission of eggs or milt. Male salmon turn a reddish colour and the bottom jaw at the nose develops a hook or gib as it is sometimes called. The female also changes colour, the colouration changing to grey and black.

Bearing these facts in mind it is always best to be absolutely sure your fish is a clean one before you kill it. A sympathetic bailiff may come along, but again the official may not be so kindly disposed. Loss of the licence and one's good name as an angler usually follows. Surely it is not worth the risk. If you are in any doubt release the fish and hope for better luck next time.

The keystone to successful salmon angling is the exercise of patience at all times. Here are what I consider to be seven faults. One or other of these is often made by a beginner resulting in freedom for the fish.

1. Striking too soon; 2. Failure of tackle when under strain; 3. Line, cast or trace too elastic to drive home the hook; 4. Failure of knots; 5. Allowing fish to thrash about in slack water; 6. Failure to select a good landing place; 7. Bad handling of net, tailer or gaff.

Salmon are notorious for their habit of following a bait or fly before speeding up to take it. The fact that the fish has taken the angler's offering is telegraphed, via the line, to the angler and if inexperienced he strikes at once. The bait is usually pulled out of the salmon's mouth and it is scared off along with others that might be in the area. If the hook should take hold it is usually not deep enough to withstand a long, drawn-out battle. When a salmon takes bait or fly it turns back to the lie from which it came. As it turns away the line will tighten steadily and then is the time to strike and thus drive home the hook, usually in the corner of the jaw, which is the one place from which a salmon cannot dislodge a hook no matter how hard he runs or fights.

Salmon are powerful and very often weighty fish so the whole of the tackle must be in perfect condition. The jamming of a line on a reel usually means a lost fish. Then again periodic inspections of the hook or hooks should be made to see that the barbs are intact and not bent over or inwards, broken off or blunted. I have lost a number of fish in past years through not doing this simple little task.

See that both your fly reel and spinning reel are kept

oiled and clean. Swivels should be oiled occasionally to keep them in working order. A swivel that turns spasmodically not only causes kinks, but can weaken a line, if not ruin it altogether. Swivels in the old days left much to be desired, but the modern ball-bearing swivel has made the art of spinning much easier. These cost a little more than the old fashioned type, but are well worth the extra money.

Failure of knots also accounts for many lost salmon so the beginner should acquaint himself with the type of knot most suitable for the fishing he is doing. Improperly-tied knots can weaken a line by as much as 40 per cent. Knot failure is often caused by impatience and the tying should never be hurried.

Issued by the manufacturers of nylon monofilament lines, most tackle shops have cards illustrating the best type of knots to use, so when purchasing a line ask for such a card, they are usually free.

If one is using a wire trace a kink or twist in it will usually cause it to snap. Always replace the wire instead of trying to straighten it out.

Today the majority of lines are made of nylon in one form or another. With certain makes of nylon there is considerable elasticity which makes driving the barb home very difficult. It is for this reason I use braided nylon when spinning for salmon as the stretch is not so great as that of monofilament. What little there is acts as something of a safety valve when the fish starts fighting.

When the battle is nearing its end steer the fish away from shallow water, particularly where there is a shingly bottom. Too often a fish thrashing about in such water can dislodge the hook and before you can get to it, the fish has wriggled to safety. Pick out a good landing place beforehand and work your fish to it.

Impatient handling of net, tailer or gaff loses many fish each season. Before you think of using one of these landing aids be perfectly sure that the fish is absolutely tired out. When it starts to roll and lies on its side that's the time to lead it over the net or to the tailer or gaff.

Always gaff a fish behind the line and never attempt

to gaff over the line. If you are using a net draw the salmon over the net and as soon as its head is over the mouth of the net lift and the salmon will slide into the folds of the net. Salmon must always be netted head first, on no account allow the net to touch its tail or it will make another break for freedom, tired out though it may be.

If using a tailer do not try to slip the wire loop into position until the fish is quite steady and when it is in place lift and the wire will grip the wrist of the salmon's tail. Once you have your salmon out of the water carry it well back on the bank before any attempt is made to kill it or remove the hook.

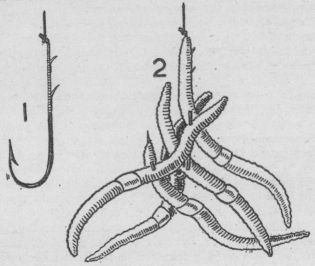

Figure 32. Salmon worm hook.
1. Round-bend salmon worm hook with whiskers of nylon whipped on to shank.
2. Baited salmon hook.

EARLY SEASON FISHING

In most parts of the country the month of February sees the opening of salmon fishing. This period of the year is usually marked by bad weather, snow, ice and floods, but few phases of angling are as intriguing as taking salmon in these conditions.

The methods of approach are slightly different from those used when the waters are normal and weather conditions more settled. For early salmon fishing, more so than at any other time the angler must be imbued with plenty of patience. You never know when the fish will come on and the angler who has his fly or bait in the water is the one, obviously who will take the fish.

Today the most common method of taking early salmon is with natural baits, such as eel-tail, sprat or minnow. On occasions when the water is very coloured a bunch of worms can be quite good. The trouble when after early season fish is that for every clean fish you hook you will hook three or four kelts (salmon that have spawned). Voracious, they will bite at anything but bear in mind what I said previously about handling such fish. Most associations have a bye-law in which the use of a gaff is prohibited during the months of February, March and April. A large mouthed net, which you would use when carp fishing, is most useful if you have a friend with you. However, if you are on your own play the fish to a standstill before slipping the net into the water. More than once I have landed salmon by playing it out then grasping the wrist of the tail with a handkerchief-wrapped hand.

For February and March you will not go far wrong if you stick to spinning an eel-tail, silver or golden sprat. These can be purchased from most tackle dealers.

The mounting of natural bait should be done carefully; remember it has to bear frequent inspection when in the water without raising suspicion. The little extra time will be well worth it. There are quite a number of good sprat tackles on the market. A spool of fine tinned copper wire or even fuse wire is needed to bind the bait to the tackle in the case of silver sprat, and for the golden variety fine copper wire is good.

With eel-tails a four inch bait is the ideal size. There are several eel-tail tackles, but my preference is for the "Geen Cork-screw" as it does away with the need for binding the bait to the tackle. The head of the tackle is weighted which makes for good casting and distance.

With all natural baits it is advisable to work the deep pools, paying particular attention to those spots where

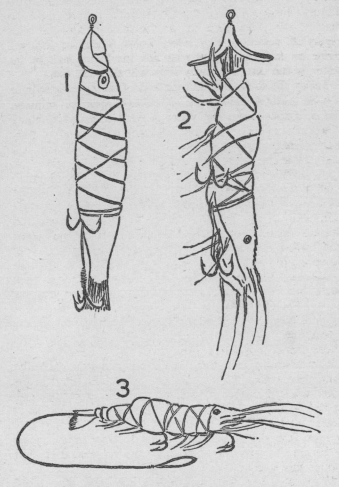

Figure 33. Natural baits mounted.
1. Sprat.
2. Prawn.
3. "The Test" Prawn tackle for use with fly-rod.

there are large sunken rocks. Towards evening deep, rocky streams can at times be quite productive.

When a salmon takes hold, play it hard and encourage it to run so as to tire quickly and whenever possible get below the fish for by so doing he is fighting the stream as well as you. With a fish straight from the sea the odds are that he will run straight down-stream and when this happens go after it if you can. Once turned it is ten to one he will make for the spot where he was hooked. If it shows signs of wanting to go down-stream again hold it back as much as possible. Unless it can run faster than the stream, the water will get behind its gills and choke it, so this again will compel it to use more energy. Keep the rod up so as to exert as much pressure as possible, but lower the rod-top if the fish jumps, this will relieve the pressure and prevent the salmon from using its weight against a tight line. As the runs get shorter put on more pressure and in a very short time you will have the battle won.

ARTIFICIAL BAITS

Some anglers I know never bother with natural baits relying on such artificials as spoons, devons and wagtails. I have caught fish on all of them, but if restricted to the use of only one type of artificial my choice would be the spoon. In recent years American type plug baits have appeared and last season a friend of mine fishing the River Wye had three salmon during a morning's fishing when using a green and yellow plug bait.

But to return to the use of a spoon bait. For early fish I prefer a two-inch plain silver spoon fastened to a three-feet 15 pound wire trace in which there is a ball-bearing swivel at the line end of the trace.

Its appeal to salmon, which by the way, are about the most curious of fish when straight from the sea, lies in its action, for not only does it spin, but it weaves an erratic course along the path the angler has chosen.

The productive casts I have found are those up and across the stream, letting the current carry the spoon, wobbling and turning until it is opposite the angler; then

116

and not before is the reel handle turned and then as slowly as possible just so that the spoon is kept from snagging the bottom.

If the pools are deep the best weight to use is a Wye lead, for it also acts as an anti-kink. Never move the spoon through the water as if you were afraid the fish would bite. Salmon usually follow a spoon some distance before striking so it is in your own interest to allow them time to make up their minds. More salmon are lost every season than gained through turning a reel handle too fast.

The idea in the make-up of a spoon is that it represents an immature fish wandering aimlessly, so wherever there is a current let it do the locomotion. In a pool minus a good current work the spoon as slowly as possible, paying particular attention to rocky areas, for it is in such places that the biggest fish lurk.

Always keep your spoons bright, for it is the flash, coupled with movement vibrations, that attract. Generally speaking I have found that the more flash one can get from a spoon during the early days of a season the more chance of success. In coloured water a spoon that has little or no flash is not going to produce very well. Later as the water fines down I usually make a change to a silver and gold spoon.

However, while I have held forth at some length on the virtues of spoon, I always go prepared and have with me a couple of three-inch devons coloured brown and gold, and yellow and green, and a plain silver, and plain gold, a total of four. If you take a lot of different baits with you a good deal of your time will be spent changing baits and in the short daylight hours of February much valuable fishing time will be lost.

TAKE AN "OTTER" WITH YOU

With metal baits that work deep down there is always present the danger that the hook will snag a rock or weeds so he is a wise angler who takes with him a bait releaser, more commonly known as an "otter". There are all sorts of bait releasers and while such a contrivance will not

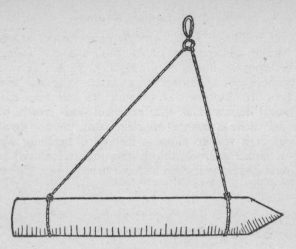

Figure 34. "Otter".

release every bait that snags it will recover a good many.

The one I usually have with me is fairly easy to make and consists of a 1½-inch thick piece of rounded wood, one foot in length and pointed at one end. It is given a couple of coats of varnish to make it water-proof. At the sharpened end a nine-inch length of string is fastened to a link swivel and the other end is connected to the swivel with a 14-inch length of string.

When a bait snags the "otter" is put on the line via the link swivel and allowed to slide down the line, point first, until it is over the spot where the bait is fast. A jerk or two on the rod top and the bait usually frees itself due to the "otter" exerting a pull through bouyancy from a different angle to that originally applied by the angler.

To conclude this section on early fishing the strength of line I favour for spinning is 15 lb. I agree that some anglers advocate a much stronger one, but having killed a number of both Atlantic and Pacific salmon of over 30 pounds each on such a line, that is the one I prefer. As to a rod, if your pike spinning rod is not too stiff you will be able to cast reasonably well, but as soon as you can afford it purchase a rod made specially for the job.

By the middle of June many rivers are so full of weed as to make spinning with metal baits a costly business. At the commencement of a season there are very few weeds about, but as the water temperature rises the weeds that have lain dormant surge with life and soon many pools and lies are thick with luxuriant weed growth, with here and there a channel of clear water. So for obvious reasons, it is well to adopt a method of spinning where loss of tackle and valuable fishing time is reduced to a minimum. Some years ago a friend of mine Roy Chilvers, the well-known Hampshire Avon angler, experimented with balsa-wood devons and plugs. The Avon is one of the most weedy rivers in the whole of the country. Indeed, many beats are never fished for salmon after June so thick does the weed become. The success Roy had tempted me to try balsa-wood baits, and from my experience, I believe that such baits can prove at least a partial answer to the weed problem.

Blanks for the making of such baits are the same as those used for the making of floats. Through the hole in the centre an aluminium or plastic tube is run, glue the outside of the tube before insertion. A balsa-wood blank is usually six inches in length and it is an easy matter to make a couple of three-inch or three two-inch ones. As the summer advances two-inch baits are quite large enough. These are armed with No. 6 tapered-shank treble hooks whipped to 20 lb. wire.

As to colour combinations I rely on three—yellow and

Figure 35. Balsa-wood Devon.

green (Yellow Belly), brown and gold and black and gold. These light-weight baits are very easy to shape with No. 300 emery paper. The spinning vanes are of celluloid, placed in slots cut with a razor-blade and glued in position.

Trace length and weight used are important factors in the successful working of these artificials. The most convenient length of trace is from 2 ft. to 2 ft. 6 in. and the weight that has done a good job for me is a three-eighth-ounce Wye lead. The weight travels near the bottom but the balsa-wood devon rises and spins on an even keel.

Balsa-wood plugs are just as easy to make. The tail-end is tapered and the head is grooved to afford a resistance to the water which starts the plug fluttering and working through the water in a zig-zag manner.

A preserved prawn is also a good bait for summer use, either as a spinning bait or worked sink-and-draw minus spinning tackle with a fly-rod.

USING A PRAWN

Spinning a prawn is similar to that when using other natural baits. The prawn is fastened to the tackle with copper wire: a three feet wire trace and a suitable Wye lead for the state of the water completes the equipment. The tail of the prawn is next to the spinning vanes and the head is at the hook end of the tackle.

Preserved prawns can be purchased from most tackle shops, but I think there is more fun if you preserve your own. Here's how:— Purchase a pint of prawns from your fishmonger and select the smallest, those from two to three inches in length; eat the larger ones yourself. Wash the selected prawns in cold water then put them, head downwards in a screw-top jar in a solution of 5 per cent formalin. They will keep for at least a twelve-month. However, the night before you go fishing take three or four of the prawns out of the preservative and let them soak in glycerine over-night, this will get rid of the formalin smell. You can preserve other natural baits in a similar way.

If you use a prawn with the fly-rod seek out those places where there is a good stream running, or spots where there are rocks in mid-stream round which the water eddies and swirls.

Assuming you have located a likely spot look around for some cover for yourself. The cast is made under-hand into the current and every inch fished by lowering the top of the rod which will send the bait down-stream a few feet at a time as you release a little line, then bring it back to the original starting point by raising the rod-top in small jerks. This way the bait will sink as the rod-top lowers and comes to the surface as it is raised. When the first few feet have been fished let out a little more line and commence all over again. Don't leave your cover until you have fished the place out.

Most prawn tackles on the market have treble hooks, but for use with a fly-rod double hooks are best, one at the head and another near the middle of the body. A tackle I can thoroughly recommend is "The Test", for once you have a model they are easy to construct at home. The needle of the tackle is pushed through the centre of the prawn and the hooks are bound in position with fine copper wire. A ten-pound nylon trace of three feet in length is what I use and this is fastened direct to the fly-line.

One interesting feature of this type of prawn fishing is that very often you can see the salmon come to within a few inches of the surface and take the prawn, and it is then that the will-power of the angler must come into play as the strike must be delayed just long enough to allow the fish to turn and head for his lie. It is when he turns that the strike must be made, for then the hooks are driven into the gristle of the jaw and not pulled out of his mouth as would be the case, as I know to my cost, if the tightening of the line was made as soon as he takes hold.

In playing a prawn-hooked salmon a tight line with very little pressure is all that is needed when he makes his first run. After that it is up to the angler to put on pressure as the occasion demands.

The methods and tackle used during the summer months can be exploited during autumn, but in times of flood and coloured water during late season it is best to revert to the baits and tactics of the spring period. However, when late season fishing bear in mind what I have said regarding near spawning fish.

FLY-FISHING FOR SALMON

Sometimes the beginner at salmon fishing is awed by the talk of experts and receives the impression that only after years of practice can he hope to catch a salmon on a fly. A few years ago salmon fly-rods were heavy and up to 18 feet in length, today, with hollow-glass, rods are much lighter and I see no reason why a 12-year-old boy or girl of reasonable physique should not take salmon on a fly. The youngster who can cast a trout fly can with little practice, produce a creditable line for salmon. It does not necessarily follow that one has to cast a long line to lure a fish, very often salmon lie close in and casts have to be made when standing back from the water's edge.

However, one thing to remember, never over-load yourself with too many fly patterns or else the time will most surely come when you will spend more time changing flies than you do fishing. I know because I went through the "grasshopper" minded stage early on in my career, fortunately the habit was arrested before it became deep-seated.

When I wrote my book on "Salmon Fishing" some years ago, my fly box contained 12 patterns, but in two sizes making 24 flies in all. Today the patterns have been reduced to six, total number of flies 12 and I still catch as many salmon as I ever did. The patterns now in my box are Durham Ranger, Blue Charm, Fiery Brown, Thunder and Lightning, Shrimp Fly and Spring Grub. The sizes are No. 4 for early season fishing whenever the water is suitable and No. 6 for summer and autumn. However, in mid-summer I have often had recourse to sea trout flies to lure a fish and the two patterns which have taken quite a few fish are Peter Ross and Bloody Butcher dressed on No. 10 hooks.

In Scotland and Ireland I have seen anglers using two flies on their leader, but that to my way of thinking is asking for trouble if you hook a fish. The runs and dives of a hooked fish are bad enough to control without worrying as to whether the second fly is going to snag.

In salmon fly fishing the angler must persevere. If you have seen a fish move work your fly where you think his lie is for at least half-an-hour, then give him a rest say for 20 minutes, put on a different fly and have another go before you move on.

As to working a fly it is curious to observe the different methods employed by anglers, I have tried many but the one that has taken the most fish is very simple. Let your fly sink fairly deep and as it swings round with the current move the rod-top slowly up and down until the cast is fished out. In water of three to four feet the fly should be worked a little faster. This movement of the rod-top imparts a semblance of life to the fly in that the wings and hackle open and shut as the fly progresses.

On fast runs, where salmon like to cruise during early morning and also in the evening, the fly will drag and be brought to the surface. On such water you will have to "mend the line". This is done by lifting the rod-top and switching the line upstream again which enables the fly to remain well down much longer. The "mend" or "switch-over" as some anglers call it is not easy to master and requires some practice, but it is well worth the time expended. It took me several weeks of practising before I could "throw" the necessary loop of line up-stream. For rocky, turbulent stretches of water it is an ideal method of exploring with the fly all the best places.

Once you have landed your first salmon on a fly you will find that fishing for them with a fly-rod casts an irresistible spell that grasps the wildest imagination so tightly that never again will you be able to free yourself of its magic fascination.

For many years now the dry-fly has been considered to be, first and foremost, a trout lure. Some years ago I experimented with it when fishing for salmon. My reason for doing so followed an incident which took me quite by surprise.

I had tried fly, spinner and prawn without any response from a salmon. As several nice trout were rising I put on a size ten Grey Palmer, dry-fly. On the fourth cast a heavy fish took. It was not a trout, but a lively 9 lb. salmon. Before that week was out that dry-fly had accounted for a couple more.

I appreciate that this method is nothing new for salmon, but it is very rarely that one comes across an angler using a dry-fly for these fish. This to my mind is a pity. The dry-fly will not take as many or as large fish as the wet-fly, but it has saved the day for me, both in this country and abroad.

During the experimental period I tried out all manner of dry-flies but the dressings which answered best were Palmers and Spiders dressed on No. 10 hooks.

When you notice a salmon cruising just beneath the surface, his presence being indicated by an occasional boil here and there, take my advice and change over to the dry-fly and it is quite possible you will connect with him.

The dry-flies I can recommend are Grey and Black Palmer and the Black and Silver Spider, also the Cinnamon Sedge. The Palmer flies are excellent for early evening fishing when the fish are moving up into the streams for oxygen and an exercise swim, spider flies and the Cinnamon Sedge are often good at mid-day.

If you have been putting in a little practice at dressing flies you should experience little difficulty in making these patterns.

FOUL-HOOKED SALMON

Occasionally you may hook a fish other than in the mouth. This usually results from the salmon turning away from the angler's offering at the last moment.

Figure 36. Dry-flies for salmon.
1. Grey Palmer.
2. Cinnamon Sedge.

Many anglers, I have no doubt, will thrill to what they believe to be a particularly vicious strike, only to discover after a long and drawn-out battle that the salmon they thought to be a very large one, is after all an ordinary one of perhaps 10 or 12 lb. hooked foul.

It has happened to me on quite a number of occasions, and will again, no doubt.

Of the salmon hooked other than in the mouth many are lost simply because the angler was "out of touch" and failed to realise that different tactics were needed under such conditions. Fish, despite what many think, are up to a point thinking creatures. They know fear and they know anger, they feel elated at times and at others depressed. By bearing these facts in mind the successful landing of a foul-hooked fish is made much easier.

Take a salmon that is hooked in the tail. Immediately he feels a brake on his normal progress he goes into top gear and streaks away on a long run, maybe he thinks that if he does not run at full stretch that which has hold of him will be able to get a better hold. He runs faster and faster, and his fear is greater than in the case of a fish normally hooked.

A fish is designed to move forward, and pressure from the angler in an effort to turn a stern-hooked fish will have little or no effect beyond making the fish strive harder to

125

get away. However, the turning of the fish becomes fairly simple. Remember the salmon is trying to shake off something that has laid violent hold of him. The angler has to make the salmon think that the enemy has been outwitted. It requires a little judgement.

When first hooked the fish is at the peak of his strength, so let him go for a 20 or 30 yard run if he wants to, under about 50 per cent, of the pressure the tackle will stand. Then, still keeping the line taut, take off the pressure, recovering the line by walking down-stream. The fish usually turns and starts to move up-stream. Let him have a few yards easy swimming, then apply the pressure once more. Away streaks the fish, pressure is relieved and back he will come. So the battle proceeds with more and more pressure being applied as the runs get shorter and weaker.

The greatest danger of losing such a fish comes at the end of a fight when the hook has pulled along the flesh and may get enough play to fall out in a moment of slack. For this reason the tail-hooked fish should be held harder than normal as he is brought stern-first to the net or gaff.

If a salmon is hooked ahead of the dorsal fin, playing follows the same pattern as if hooked in the mouth. The difference is that any strong pressure from the angler will set the fish crosswise. The salmon must be worked in against or at least across the flow, and that means a lot of leg work as the fish moves down- and up-stream.

A belly-hooked fish is a difficult one to handle in that only the slightest pressure can be applied for more than three-parts of the fight. Any strong pull on the part of the angler will usually make the fish roll over and over, with a resultant heavy strain on the terminal tackle. The full strength of the rod should only be exerted when the fish shows definite signs of exhaustion, then it becomes an easy matter to bring him in to net or gaff.

With all foul-hooked salmon a taut line at all times is essential to success. The largest River Tweed salmon I ever landed, a 29-pounder, was hooked in the belly near the vent. It kept me busy for near two hours and when gaffed the hook just fell out of the two-inch gash it had made. This proved I had put on far too much pressure, and if I had lost the fish it would have been my own fault. That was over 30 years ago. Today I know better.

I hope what I have written about salmon will tempt you to try your luck. Of course this chapter should be looked upon as a foundation upon which the young angler can build and develop through his own experiences and by watching others trying to lure the King of Game Fish.

9

Fly-dressing know-how

THE art of fly-dressing remains a deep mystery to many ardent anglers. Why it remains as such is indeed the greatest mystery for artificial flies are simple to construct, requiring only a few tools, a handful of assorted feathers, various tinsels, wools, furs, floss silk and tying silk, together with a few minutes of your spare time. Any boy or girl from the age of nine onwards can dress flies and don't think it takes years to learn how to do it. Chances are that the first fly you attempt will surprise you in its appearance and in its ability to catch fish. There are only two knots to bother about, the half-hitch and whip finish.

In the early days of my career as a newspaper reporter (journalist) salaries were very small, so having been taught how to dress flies by my parents, I augmented my pocket money by becoming a professional fly-dresser. The whole of my spare time, when not at the office, was devoted to turning out flies for a number of tackle shops.

But to return to the subject matter. What is necessary so that you can dress your own flies? First, a vice is required to hold the hook securely, allowing you to have both hands free to work. There are numerous vices available, most being very inexpensive, but get one that will hold small as well as large hooks. A pair of small scissors which will have long sharp points is another handy tool. Still another which is helpful, especially when dressing dry-flies, is a pair of hackle pliers. You will also require a bottle of clear nail varnish to finish off the heads of your flies and a piece of fly-dresser's wax.

Those named are the bare essential tools. Not as many to acquire as you may have suspected. As for feathers if you know someone who keeps poultry then you will have a ready source of supply when requiring hackle feathers from the necks of cocks and hens. This is as good a place

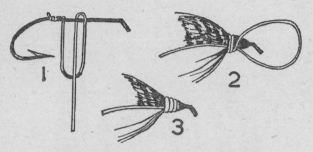

Figure 37. Half-hitch and whip-finish knots.
1. Half-hitch knot.
2. Start of whip-finish knot at head of fly.
3. The completed whip-finish knot.

as any to mention that for wet-flies the hackle feathers used are from hens and those for dry-flies are from cocks. Once sure of the rudiments all you will need is practice, so by word and illustration I will try to explain how to dress a wet spider trout fly, a winged sea trout fly, Streamer fly, hair-winged trout fly and my old friend the Blue Charm salmon fly.

THE WET SPIDER FLY

I am often asked what I consider to be the best all round type of wet fly for trout, and on each occasion that this query has been voiced I have had no hesitation in naming the Spider.

Strangely enough this creation of the fly-dresser's art has no outward resmblance to one of Nature's works, but it scores because of its life-like action when in the water.

Of course there are spiders and spiders. Some offered

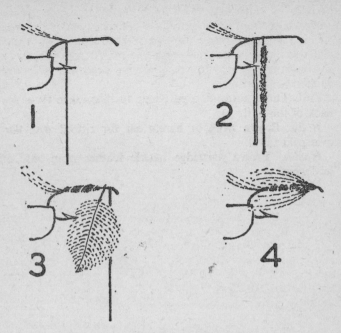

Figure 38. March Brown Spider (wet).

1. Three fibres of a partridge feather are tied in for the tail.
2. A length of fine oval gold tinsel is waiting to be wound round body and brown wool has been spun on to the tying silk.
3. Body is complete and a partridge hackle feather is ready to be wound at head.
4. The finished fly.

for sale are far too heavily dressed with the result that the fly is dense and practically opaque. Cut down on the density of the hackle and the light filters through to give the artificial a translucency which characterises most natural insects.

Another fact that must appeal to all teenage enthusiasts is the fact that this artificial is the most simple of all to dress. In the main it consists of body material and a small hen hackle or that from some other bird wound at the head. Some spiders have two or three fibres from a hackle feather for the tail.

Naturally there are hundreds of different spider patterns but one I prefer above all others when after early trout is the March Brown. However, like many trout flies there are variations in its dressing, the one given here is in my opinion the best.

Tail: Three fibres of a partridge feather taken from the back of the bird.

Body: Brown wool or hare's ear fur ribbed with fine oval gold tinsel.

Hackle: Brown partridge hackle feather from base of bird's neck.

Tying silk: Yellow.

Hooks: No. 14-16 or 18.

The accompanying sketches (figure 38) illustrate each step in the making of this pattern and if followed carefully no teenager should experience any difficulty in turning out a decent looking fly. However, I repeat, only practice will enable you to produce the works of art you see displayed in tackle shops.

SPIDER DRY-FLIES

In the case of dry-fly spiders the same technique is followed, but instead of a soft-fibred hackle being used at the head you use a stiff-fibred cock hackle. After much experimenting I found that the type of feather which is ideal for numbers 14, 16 and 18 hooks is that found near the top of a cockerel's neck. These particular feathers are small and stiff and are minus webbing (soft fibres). Remember this type of fly balances on the tips of the hackle and tail. A soft fibred tail or hackle would be useless in this respect.

MALLARD AND CLARET, SEA TROUT FLY

Just as the March Brown spider is excellent for trout so is the Mallard and Claret one of the best patterns for sea trout. Wherever there are sea trout you will find anglers pinning their faith in this winged wet-fly. It is also a good pattern for trout when fishing lochs or reservoirs.

Figure 39. Mallard and Claret sea trout fly.

1. Tail of golden pheasant tippet is tied in, a length of fine oval gold tinsel is waiting to be wound and some claret wool has been spun on to the tying silk.
2. Body is complete and a claret hen hackle is waiting to be wound.
3. Hackle is in position.
4. The finished fly with brown mallard wings.

Tail: Three fibres from the tippet feather of a golden pheasant.

Body: Claret wool or seal's fur ribbed with fine oval gold tinsel.

Hackle: Claret coloured hen hackle.

Wings: Brown mallard.

Tying silk: Claret.

Hooks: No. 8, 10 or 12 for sea trout and No. 14 for trout.

BLACK GHOST STREAMER FLY

For the novice this is about the easiest of all streamer flies to dress.

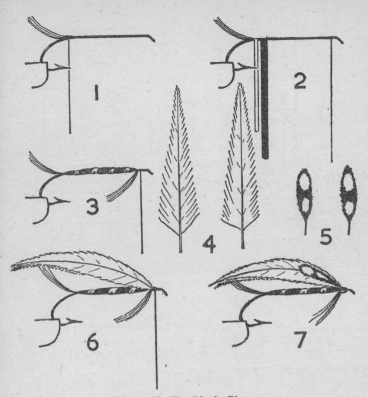

Figure 40. The Black Ghost.

1. The tail of golden pheasant topping feather fibres is tied in place.
2. Lengths of silver tinsel and black floss silk are waiting to be wound to form body.
3. Body is complete and the throat hackle of golden pheasant topping has been tied in.
4. Two white cock hackle feathers for the wings.
5. Two jungle cock feathers for the cheeks.
6. The wings are in position.
7. The completed fly.

Tail: Golden pheasant topping feather.

Body: Black floss silk, ribbed with broad oval silver tinsel.

Hackle: Golden pheasant topping feather, tied beneath shank.

Wings: Two white cock hackles.
Cheeks: Jungle cock.
Tying silk: Black.
Hooks: No. 8, 10 or 12, long-shanked Mayfly. Numbers 8 and 10 hooks are for sea trout and No. 12 for trout.

HAIR-WINGED FLY (WET)

As I mentioned earlier hair from various animals is now being used extensively in the "winging" of both wet- and dry-flies, indeed, the day may not be far distant when feather wings will be a thing of the past. From my experience, providing hair is used sparingly it is an excellent material. When it is thick and bunched together it is not long before the hair becomes matted with the result that the fine filaments can no longer "breathe" as it were. Sparse hair wings on a wet-fly in the water move in and out as movement is imparted to it by water current or the angler. It is these delicate wing movements that intrigue the fish and give "life" to the artificial.

Hair from the tail of a grey squirrel is ideal for the "winging" of all sorts of wet-flies, what is more it can be dyed any colour you like. To give some idea of the versatility of squirrel hair, a friend of mine uses nothing else for the wings of trout, sea trout and salmon flies.

The dressing given below was invented by my fishing friend Jim Warne, who is head bailiff of the Brockenhurst Fly-fishing Club on the Lymington River (Hampshire). He has named it "Squirrel Grey".

Tail: Three or four hairs from a grey squirrel tail.
Body: Grey wool or seal's fur, ribbed with fine gold oval tinsel, the wool to be teased out between the ribbing.
Wings: Grey squirrel.
Tying silk: Grey.
Hooks: No. 14 and 16 for trout and No. 10 and 12 for sea trout.

Before passing on, there are a couple of things to bear in mind. With fur or wool bodies see that your tying silk is well waxed, so that when you work the material onto the tying silk with your thumb and forefinger it will adhere.

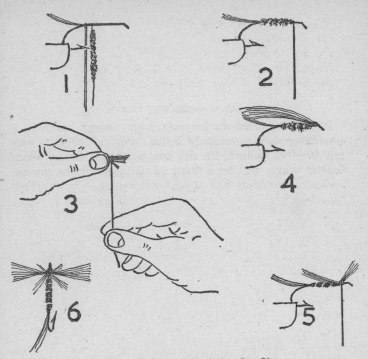

Figure 41. Wet and dry hair-wing flies.

1. Tail of squirrel hair is tied in, a length of gold tinsel is hanging and some grey wool is on tying silk.
2. The body is complete.
3. A sparse bunch of squirrel hair is tied in.
4. The finished fly.
5. Putting hair-wings on a dry-fly.
6. A finished hair-wing dry-fly.

Secondly after you have cut off the amount of hair you require for the wings put a spot of clear nail varnish on the roots, this will keep the hair together while you are tying it in and will make a more secure job.

HAIR-WING DRY-FLY

Dry-flies with hair-wings are just as simple to create as wet-flies. The famous American fly-dresser Lee Wulff some years ago invented a number of various dry-flies

135

the most famous being the Grey Wulff, Brown Wulff and Red Wulff; all have squirrel wings. In Hampshire the Grey Wulff is deadly during the Mayfly season and the Red Wulff has lured large numbers of rainbow trout and several salmon.

Squirrel tails can be purchased from most tackle shops dealing in fly-dressing materials, in natural or dyed colours.

It will readily be seen in the sketches how easy hair-wing patterns are to make, for wet- or dry-flies.

BLUE CHARM SALMON FLY

This pattern has a pretty name, is easy to dress and can, with the utmost confidence, be used right through the season. At the age of 15 my youngest daughter Marion caught a couple of salmon on a Blue Charm she dressed herself, while fishing the River Wye. Since then it has been her favourite fly and the hook size she prefers is a No. 6 whether the water is coloured or clear.

It is also one of my firm favourites and each year I manage to lure a fish or two on it.

Here then is the dressing of this all-purpose fly: —

Tag: Silver wire and gold floss silk, four turns each.

Tail: Golden pheasant topping feather.

Butt: Black ostrich herl.

Body: Black floss silk, ribbed oval silver tinsel.

Throat hackle: Blue.

Wings: Brown mallard or dark brown speckled turkey tail and a narrow strip of teal on top with a golden pheasant topping over all.

Head: Black varnish.

Tying silk: Black.

Hooks: No. 4 or 6.

In conclusion, if this brief chapter has whetted your appetite, I shall have achieved what I set out to do, that is to have most young fly-fishermen dressing their own flies. Practice will smooth out little difficulties and in less than three months you will be dressing flies that will lure trout, sea trout and salmon. There are a number of books

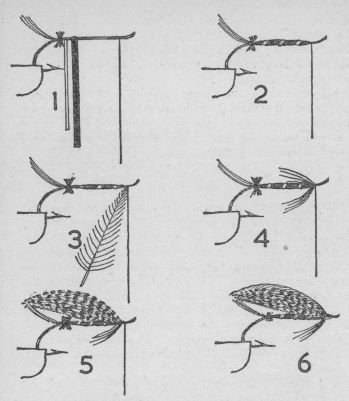

Figure 42. Blue Charm salmon fly.

1. The tag, butt and tail are in position and lengths of oval silver tinsel and black floss silk are ready to form the body.
2. Body is complete.
3. Blue hen hackle is ready to be wound, three turns only.
4. Hackle is in position.
5. Wings of brown mallard or brown speckled turkey with a narrow strip of teal on top are in place.
6. The finished fly with golden pheasant topping feather over all and black varnish head.

on the subject of fly-dressing, indeed, some years ago I wrote one myself and in it you will find the dressings of all the most famous gamefish flies. (*Fly Dressing and Some Tackle Making, published by Elliot Right Way Books*).

10
Sea Angling

THERE comes a time in the lives of many teenagers dwelling inland when they want to go down to the sea with rod and reel. They want to experience the novelty of saltwater angling, to pit their skill against the ocean's varied fighters, to catch something they have never before landed, and so these youngsters get tackle together, and with (or without!) their parents head for the coast.

To the young angler schooled in freshwater or game fishing, nothing is so impressive and at the same time so discouraging to the beginner, say at beach fishing, as the size of the potential fishing ground. The vastness of the sea stretching out to the horizon appears devoid of any means of locating fish. There are none of the familiar guides which are associated with good fishing places. There are no visible weed beds around which a bait can be cast, in fact, it would seem that to capture a fish in the wide expanses of the ocean could only be a pure matter of chance. Yet, there are any number of signposts which point the way to successful beach-fishing, and only by recognising these can the young angler graduate from the novice class into the realms of the accomplished angler.

As in all angling, the only way a beginner can hope to achieve success is by a combination of keen perception and a willingness to "learn" the surf. The initial impression in which the shore-line appears to stretch out smoothly for miles is a very deceptive one as it gives little indication that the floor of inshore waters are pocketed with little hills and valleys each of which may represent possible feeding grounds for inshore bound fish.

Most of the fish found near beaches feed on a wide variety of baits that are fairly easy to come by and include shell-fish such as mussels, cockles and razor-fish; crustaceans like crab and shrimp; worms (lug and rag); fish-flesh such as sprat, sand-eel, herring, mackerel, squid and a host of others. Crustaceans shell-fish and the fry of other fish will most often be found where the surging currents have washed out hiding places, or in backwaters and racing eddies—seeking refuge from the advancing tide.

With this in mind the prospective beach-fisherman can at once begin to locate possible feeding grounds. Casting any old where, believe me, is the right way to end the day with an empty bag.

The first lesson which the newcomer has to learn is one of geography—the geography of the ocean bottom in the places to be fished. Here the saltwater angler possesses an invaluable ally which is not available in freshwater. The daily rise and fall of the tides allow the beach-angler to see the fishing area under all conditions.

Exploratory trips along the shore at very low tides will disclose a panorama quite different from the impression gained by scanning the surface at high tide. Here for example, is a deep trough between outer bar and shore where small fish dart about and crabs scramble over the bottom in search of food as the tide begins to ebb. Surely this is a good mark for fishing when the tide starts to rise. Yonder is a deep cut between two sand-bars where currents rushing out of the tidal pools dash head-long into the foaming breakers.

WHAT THE WAVES TELL

Of course, it might be said that not everyone has the time or opportunity to indulge in such scouting expeditions, yet if you are observant, the waves themselves will disclose much of the same information. Waves do not break upon the shore in a completely symmetrical manner in most cases.

139

The apparent "sameness" of each breaker as it builds up and with increasing speed reaches a crest to dash on the beach is rarely typical of existing conditions. In one place the combers will break some distance off-shore and tell of a hidden sand-bar below. Another section will reveal that the waves do not crest until reaching the beach —many times indicating a deep hole in that spot.

Tide-rips where two or more currents join in a medley of whirlpools and white water often mark an unusual convolution of the bottom where fish come to feed on the food whirled about in the racing seas.

Among the obvious good places to fish are where rivers empty into the sea. In the spring river mouths are the gate-ways through which small fish travel on the way to shallow spawning grounds. Each incoming tide brings more hosts and it is not long before large fish begin to concentrate in such places. Later on as the spent (spawned) fish return to the sea, new schools of large fish congregate for the feast.

Another "hot-spot" for a new-comer is a jetty. These wooden or rock promontories have long been favoured spots of mine. The area in the vicinity of a jetty's foundations becomes a veritable aquarium of sea life as crabs, mussels, barnacles, and worms take up residence nearby. These creatures attract myriads of small fish which come to feed and to hide within the boundaries of the submerged obstruction. The cycle of sea life then progresses as the larger fish are attracted by this easy to get at food.

BEST TIDE

Opinions on the best tide for beach-casting run through the full stages of the tide both incoming and outgoing. One old angler swears by high-water; another holds the view that the first of the ebb is best; still a third avers that the best fishing may be enjoyed just as the currents turn and the water begins to rise. Actually there is no "best" tide as there are numerous other factors which affect the feeding habits of any fish.

Clearness of the water, temperature, amount of available food, wind direction; all these and many more affect the behaviour of fish. Each section of coastline has certain local conditions that may make a stage of the tide best at some times.

For example, fishing around the mouth of a river is often considered best when the tide is falling. During this period the brackish water is emptying a constant stream of food of all kinds into the surf.

Rocks that are half exposed at low tide should be a prime target during an incoming tide. Regarding the proper tide it can only be said that the angler must become familiar with the prevailing conditions of the places to be fished. Most ardent beach-fishermen seem to agree that some movement of the tide is desirable as it stirs the bottom and moves fish food about.

GOOD FISHING WEATHER

The condition described by sea captains as "dirty weather" seems to fit the ideal time for beach-casting quite well. Choppy seas with white water lashing the beaches is the ideal time for seeking fish in the surf. This is completely contrary to what the beginner would expect. One look at the angry seas is usually a sufficient convincer that no fish could or would possibly be found within miles of the shore.

Yet, this is quite often opposite to actual conditions, for the rough and tumble fighters of the surf such as bass like nothing better than to feed on the food which is churned about at such times.

Of course, this is not inviolate as there are times when a calm day or night will produce excellent fishing, but in general it might be said that on those days when all judgement indicates settling down in front of a warm fire with a good book, beach-casting is most likely to be productive.

Perhaps it is the uncertainty of never knowing what will strike the bait or it might be some deep-rooted urge that compels the angler to go down to face one of Nature's mightiest forces. Whatever the reason, casting from the beaches has long attracted fishermen of all ages and each year enrolls growing numbers of enthusiasts. It is a fascinating sport, often thrilling and in terms of fish taken can often be a most rewarding one. Beach-casting is basic and completely alive and because of these qualities it is most appealing to young people who hate to be fettered with all manner of rules and regulations.

INSHORE WATER FISH

Many species of fish visit inshore waters, but the ones most likely to be caught from a beach include bass, pout whiting, flat fish such as plaice, sole and flounder, mackerel and the occasional skate and conger eel. In winter schools of cod and whiting make their appearance.

TACKLE REQUIRED

You will need a beach-casting rod, this you can make yourself from blanks or purchase ready made, but take my advice and get hollow fibre-glass. A large type fixed spool-reel is much better than a multiplyer to start off with for the simple reason you do not have to worry about over-runs. Your line can be braided nylon or nylon mono-filament, but it should not be less than 18 lb. breaking strain. Don't worry about long casting for that will come with practice, indeed, on steep sloping beaches a cast of thirty or forty yards will often be found to be quite adequate.

You will want a number of lead weights to aid in casting and to suit the various states of the tide, some swivels and hooks; as to terminal tackle we will talk about that later.

FROM PIER AND HARBOUR WALL

On most piers and harbours one can hire tackle and purchase suitable bait as well. The observant teenager visiting a pier or harbour can learn a great deal from watching and listening to the old-timers. Of course one advantage that can be claimed for this kind of fishing is, that it is as a rule, carried out without professional assistance, with the result that for any success that he attains the angler must rely on his own skill.

For giving the novice ideas on the subjects of bait, tackle, rods and tides and the many other facts that affect sport, pier or harbour fishing is, I think, most useful and will produce a far more efficient and finished article than the angler who goes boat fishing and relies mainly on the boatman. I have often thought for this reason that a certain amount of pier and harbour wall fishing forms an excellent training, but it must be taken first, for the difference in results is so great that once one does much boat fishing, shore, pier and harbour angling is pushed into the background.

ESTUARY FISHING

The interesting thing about an estuary is that it is one of the most productive areas during spring, summer and autumn for such species as sea trout, grey mullet, bass and flounders. As the water temperature rises other species also find their way there. Some anglers seem to think that an estuary is a sort of barren no-man's land, believe me, nothing could be farther from the truth.

The estuary fisherman's bible is the tide tables, but it is fairly easy to work them out for yourself once you have ascertained the age of the moon. Spring tides begin two tides before the new and full moon and continue for four days after, the neap tides begin with the second tide before the first and last quarters of the moon, the slackest being in the third tide. The neap tides end 60 hours later; thus the period between the highest tide and the lowest is roughly eight days.

Most estuary fish move in and out with the tides, except the flounder which usually buries itself in the sand as the tide ebbs, coming out again to forage as it starts to run. Therefore the angler should be in position before the tide starts to make. However, before he sets up his tackle he should have taken a walk at slack water and memorised the likely fish haunts. Sea trout love rocky channels and rarely move in mid-stream. Bass and grey mullet delight in quiet bays near storm-water over-flows and sewage outlets. If in his walk rocks and wooden pilings which are covered with sea-moss are located that is where a school of grey mullet is likely to be. These fish although delightful to eat, are, I am sorry to say, scavengers and the largest specimens are always to be found near a sewage outlet. Flounders delight in places that are a mixture of mud and sand.

For the best sport of all, night fishing is much superior to daytime. Specimen mullet do a great deal of their feeding after dark. The bass is also a night feeder, but for sea trout a moonless night is best. Before you can go after this game fish you will need to get a licence.

Flounders appear to feed best from about half-way to flood to about mid-ebb. The best period of the year, I have found by experience, is from April to October.

A CLOSER LOOK

Now let us look at each fish, taking the sea trout first. The tackle needed is a fly-rod and reel and a spinning rod and reel complete with spare drum. For daytime spinning a 7 lb. line is heavy enough, but when night falls change drums and use a 12 lb. line, for salmon usually run with a night tide to the end of the tidal water. Then, if the water of the river is suitable, they carry on, if not, they fall back to the deep sea pools. I have had quite a few salmon when sea trout spinning at night, but I repeat, don't forget to get your game fish licence before you start fishing.

I like a one-inch plain silver or silver and gold spoon for night work. For flies I have found a combination of black and silver to be best. Black wings and silver body, no tail or hackle, in making the body use silver Lurex as this plastic does not tarnish in brackish water.

For mullet close inshore the fly-rod can be used, but for distance work the spinning rod and fixed spool reel is best with a line of 5 lb. The grey mullet has a very small mouth so the hook and bait must correspond. A

No. 10 Crystal is excellent for bread or macaroni paste and for other baits such as worms a No. 8 Round Bend will be found to be best.

Mullet can be attracted by use of cloud bait, made up of crushed oat-meal biscuits worked into a paste. Before starting to fish throw in a lump of paste about the size of a walnut, it will disintegrate in the water and the minute fragments will attract the mullet without feeding them. When you see the fish moving about fix up your float

Figure 43.   Estuary sea trout fly on No. 8 hook.

tackle and use macaroni paste on your hook and it should not be long before you are in business.

If the estuary is carrying a lot of freshwater due to flooding in the river you will find that mullet stay near the bottom. Then the only way to entice a fish or two is to ledger for them. Use a No. 8 Round Bend hook upon which is impaled a two-inch piece of rag-worm. However, no matter what technique is used never let the line become taut; have a couple of yards hanging slack in the rings and when the line begins to draw out quickly, strike by lifting the rod-top smartly.

Estuaries both big and small are rich in fish food and are probably the most rewarding of all fishing grounds for the bass angler. The best tide is a spring as the extra volume of water uncovers more food than a neap one does in an estuary.

The best baits (natural) that I know are soft or peeler crab, sand-eel and rag-worm in that order; artificial baits include spoons and devons.

The movements of bass in brackish water are controlled by the action of the tides. They enter an estuary with a rising tide first in the main channel, then, as the water rises spread out over the flats. They ascend a good distance, but as soon as the tide turns they run back down again to the open sea. But throughout a season, you will find small bass in residence right through the length of the estuary. Anglers call them school bass, and they range in weight from half-pound to a pound.

Ledgering with crab or rag-worm is a good method when the tide is reaching the flood stage, but some of my largest bass have fallen to the lure of a live sand-eel fished on float tackle. Against such a bait that is moving around, the bass will charge fearlessly and will engulf it, invariably hooking himself.

The hook should be a No. 8 long shank. It is put up through the protruding bottom jaw of the bait and then brought down and pushed through the loose skin below the pelvic or ventral fin. I agree that a No. 8 hook is small, but it bites deep and will stay put despite the many twists and turns of a hooked fish.

The hook trace must be just long enough to keep the bait moving about a foot off the bottom and the best weight to use when float fishing is a Jardine Spiral. The beauty of this type of lead is that one can change it so easily for one that is lighter or heavier as the case might be. The thing to remember is that to be successful the eel must move around and a weight that prevents this is next to useless.

When dead, sand-eels are good as ledger baits in places where there is a sand-bar. Spinning with a dead sand-eel in areas where there are currents will also lure good bass. With a spinning bait, natural or artificial the angler can cover a lot of ground. The baits should be worked sink and draw, that is, once the cast has been made, time should be allowed for the bait to sink well down and then it should be retrieved with three or four turns of the handle, a slight pause, say three or four seconds and then repeat the operation until the cast is fished out.

One point to remember whenever you go after bass; exercise the utmost care when removing the hook from the fish. The gill covers of the bass are armed with small spines which can inflict a nasty wound if handled care-

Figure 44. Flounder spoon.

lessly, and the second dorsal fin with its sharp points, can also prove dangerous if the fish is mishandled. I use a leather gauntlet glove when night fishing.

We now come to the flounder, a species that spends most of its time in brackish water. It is in estuaries that have a bottom mixture of sand and mud that the largest congregations will be found.

When I started sea fishing the recognised method, was ledgering or float fishing with rag or lugworm. Then Mr. J. P. Garrad discovered that flounder could be taken in large numbers on a baited spoon. Today it is rare that I use other than the spoon when after flounder. The spoon is not intended as a bait, its purpose being that of an attractor. Flounder spoons can be purchased at most tackle shops and once you have a pattern are easy to make at home out of sheet copper or brass. A spoon three inches in length is not too large. Indeed a friend of mine who fishes the estuaries that flow into the Hampshire Solent, uses five-inch ones and catches large numbers of flounders each year. A look at the accompanying sketch gives the general idea of such a spoon. The single hook is baited with either lug or ragworm.

It was invented originally as a technique for boat fishing, but it can be used from the banks of an estuary or harbour wall. Spinning rod and fixed spool reel and a seven-pound line are what you need. Take care to see that the spoon works deep in the water. Slow recovery is one of the key-notes to success and when you feel a bite stop reeling in; this will allow the flounder to get the worm into his mouth. Then when you feel a sharp tug on your line lift your rod-top smartly and the fish will be well hooked in the mouth.

If there is a strong tide running you may have to add a little weight to keep the spoon down; use the Jardine Spiral which I referred to earlier on.

As to the colour of spoons I have found that in coloured water highly polished brass produces well and during periods of clear water a silver-coloured one is best. For deep water areas a plain white spoon is an excellent attractor.

Here is how I make my flounder spoons. The copper or brass sheeting is $\frac{1}{32}$ of an inch thickness, and after shaping with a round-headed hammer I tin it all over with ordinary solder for a silver spoon. The solder is polished to make it bright and then given a couple of coats of clear nail varnish. The size drill bit used for making the hole in the spoon is one eighth of an inch. The split ring is put on together with two small swivels. Let one hang on the inside of the spoon and to this fasten a six-inch length of 7 lb. nylon to which the hook has been attached. The hook should hang about three inches below the spoon. The line is fastened to the other swivel.

A friend of mine, rather than bother to make his own spoons, visits jumble sales and purchases for a few coppers old dessert spoons, these he converts into flounder spoons by cutting off the handles and drilling a hole in the pointed end. He catches quite a few nice flounders each season.

He also purchases smaller spoons which he converts into spoons for bass, pollack, salmon and sea trout. My friend's 14-year-old son using one of these converted spoons took his largest pike, a fish of 18 lb. when fishing the Hampshire Avon, near Fordingbridge, a few days before I wrote this chapter. So if you cannot get hold of sheet metal start converting a few old spoons.

11

Collecting your own baits

WHEN I was a teenager half the fun in sea angling was the phase that preceded the actual fishing—collecting bait. One can purchase mackerel and herring from the fishmonger's and usually squid from tackle shops near the sea. However, there are quite a number of baits, and good ones at that, which one can find on a beach or along the banks of an estuary.

The most popular of sea-shore baits are lug and rag-worm. The former lives in a mixture of sand and mud and the latter in the sticky mud and sand of estuaries, creeks, bays and harbours.

Nearly every beach and sandy estuary has its lugworm colony, which is easily located at low water by the characteristic casts left on the surface by the burrowing worms. They lie about nine inches below the surface and the best tool to use for digging them out is a garden fork. You will also need a wooden box with a handle, to carry them from place to place. This you can make at home quite easily. A box 14 inches in length, 8 inches wide and five inches deep will accommodate well over 100 worms quite comfortably. A layer of sea-weed is put in the bottom, some worms on top, another layer of weed, then worms and so on. They will keep about two or three days. However, if you can dig fresh bait each day so much the better, for flat fish in particular prefer freshly-dug worms, what is more they stay on the hook much better. Never mix lug and ragworms together for the ragworms will quickly kill the others.

When digging the object is to get a good "face" on the hole or trench removing only a few inches of sand at a time, thus the worms are exposed to view and can be picked out without damaging them. The worms congregate fairly close together so if too big a slice of sand or mud is taken many worms will be buried by the fall, what is more the vibrations set up will have alarmed all the worms in that vicinity and they will go deeper.

There is one very important factor in the keeping of all sea worms over 24 hours, the stock should be looked over each day and any dead or unhealthy looking worms removed. Dead worms will quickly contaminate and kill the others.

RAGWORM

Though the lug is very popular with beach anglers I personally much prefer the ragworm, for it is tougher and has plenty of movement when on the hook. Further it is much easier to keep for a day or two being more tenacious of life.

However, digging ragworm is a very dirty business and wellington or thigh boots are necessary. If you proceed along the same lines as that used for lugworm you should experience little difficulty. Flounders are particularly fond of freshly-dug ragworms and I believe that is one of the main reasons why they haunt estuaries and creeks.

SHELL-FISH

Mussels, cockles and slipper limpets are a trio of excellent baits and are usually quite easy to collect.

Mussels are found all round our coasts, often in very large beds. They can be found attached to the piles of piers, jetties and groynes and rocks—in fact any place that provides something firm to which they can attach themselves.

Fishing from a boat when long casting is not necessary, there is no better bait for codling than freshly-opened mussel. The best way of opening it is to take the mussel in the left hand, with the straighter edge of the shell turned away from the body. By pressing with the thumb upon the upper portion of the shell in an outward direction an opening is made into which the blade of a knife will readily enter. The greatest care must be taken to keep the knife close up to the shell when a stroke first to the right and then to the left will enable you to lift out the mussel intact.

Mussels are a very soft bait, but if you soak them in

Figure 45. Mussels and cockles.
1. Mussels on rock.
2. Cockles fresh dug from the sand.

brine (salt and water) three or four hours before using they will toughen up and stay on the hook much better.

COCKLES

This shellfish likes to hide in clean sand near the low-water mark, it is not so abundant on our beaches as the mussel, but it is an excellent bait for most bottom feeding fish. They are just as easy to open as mussels. All you have to do is get two cockles holding one in either hand with the shell joints locking against one another then give a sharp twist and the shells are open. Run a knife blade round the flesh and you have your bait. Here again we have a soft bait, but immersion in a brine bath will remedy this. Whenever I propose to use either of the baits mentioned I take them out of their shells the day before and after they have been brine-treated put them in a screw-top jar to await use. They will keep about a week with this treatment.

SLIPPER LIMPET

This shellfish is an invader from America and was first noted on the beaches near Southampton just before the first World War. It is on record that ships in ballast from America before loading emptied their ballast of shingle which came from an American beach overboard. This shingle contained slipper limpets. They had survived the long journey across the Atlantic and when dumped at Southampton found the conditions to their liking and are now well established all along the south coast and are now progressing up the east side.

Unlike the common limpet they do not attach themselves to rocks. One will attach itself to an empty mussel, winkle or other shell, even seaweed, and once a hold has been found others will lock on to the shell of the first, making bunches of a dozen or more. At low tide on southern beaches it is quite easy to collect a couple of hundred. If placed in a polythene bag as they are they will keep for several days.

They are not difficult to break apart, all you have to do

153

is twist one from the other and a knife will release the creature inside. When the shell is emptied it is easy to see why they are called "slipper" limpets. The interior of the shell is like a slipper with the toe pressed in.

The slipper limpet is a reasonably good bait for the smaller species of bottom feeding fish. A friend who does quite a lot of night fishing from his boat at Lymington (Hampshire) catches a good many sole each year on it. It is not a large bait and two or three on a hook makes an appetising morsel for the fish.

Figure 46. Limpet baits.
1. Common limpet adhering to piece of flint.
2. Little colony of slipper limpets growing together on a piece of rock.

COMMON LIMPET

This species is not often used by anglers, but I have heard that professional fishermen have had success with it when baiting their long-lines. However, I often collect them from the rocks and use them as ground-bait when seeking cod and whiting.

SOFT AND PEELER CRAB

When crabs get too large for their shells they have to shed them and once they have lost their armour-plating, as it were, they become most vulnerable to such fish as bass, pollack, skate and conger. When they feel the urge to shed their shell, crabs creep into rocky holes, or under seaweed hoping to escape the notice of the predators.

When the crab has lost its shell it is known as a "soft crab" and when about to lose it anglers refer to it as a "peeler" because you can peel the hard shell away leaving the soft one underneath.

Estuaries, bays and creeks are productive areas to hunt for them. The tool which I shall mention later on for scraping sand-eels out of the sand is ideal for hooking the crabs out of their hides.

HERMIT CRAB

This crustacean is a tasty bite for all kinds of fish. Wherever there are whelks there you will find this soft bodied crab. Don't try to pull the crab out of the shell or you will ruin it. Break the whelk shell and you can then extricate the crab. In their shells among damp seaweed they will keep quite well for a week. If on the small side you can use the crab whole, on the large side it is best to break off the body and use only that as bait. Large plaice are very partial to the body of a hermit crab.

SHRIMPS AND PRAWNS

Both these baits are ideal for use with float tackle when after bass and are easily collected with a very fine meshed net. However, to keep them alive you will need a bucket or other receptacle, because they must be kept in water. Estuary sea trout like shrimps, and on quite a few occasions when after bass I have been pleasantly surprised to hook a sea trout. When dead they can be used as ledger baits or broken up for ground-bait, when fishing from an anchored boat.

SAND-EELS

On more than one occasion I have been asked: "What is the best bait for big bass, pollack and coalfish?" Each time my answer has been the same—-sand-eel. Indeed, I think it is fairly safe to say there have been more bass, pollack and coalfish over 10 lb. taken on this bait than any other.

Although travelling about in large schools, they are not always easy to find. The professional uses a fine meshed seine net, but for the angler who wants, maybe, a couple of dozen baits now and then, the purchase of a net would be money wasted. However, once you have located a sandy beach frequented by these little fish whose proper name is "Launce", it is, with the right tool, a fairly easy matter to collect what you want.

Let us look at the subject a little more closely. In the accompanying sketch Fig. 1 is the hook for scraping in the sand and its overall length is 18 inches. The one I have used for many years is made out of a 12-inch length of one-inch steel rod which was shaped and tapered by a blacksmith friend in the days when there were plenty of horses about. The six-inch handle was fashioned from a piece of ordinary broom shank.

Wait until low water, then begin scraping to a zig-zag pattern, see Fig. 47. The eels are just below the surface of the sand at the water's edge. They settle in colonies and once you have uncovered one, your task will be easy. A word of warning—Nature in her wisdom has equipped this little fish with extraordinary powers of burrowing, so immediately you have got one out of its burrow, lift it quickly, but gently, and put it into a sea-water filled container.

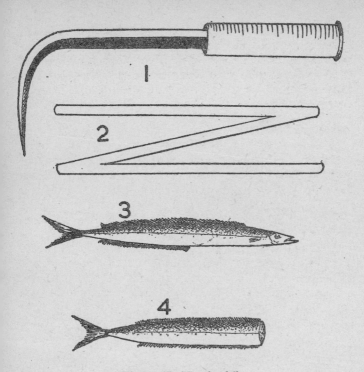

Figure 47. "Sand-eels".
1. Rake-hook for getting the "eels" out of the sand.
2. Zig-zag method of raking the sand.
3. "Sand-eel".
4. "Sand-eel" with head and shoulders cut off is an excellent
   spinning bait for salmon, mackerel, bass, pollack and
   coalfish.

In Fig. 3 we have a sketch of a sand-eel and in the
next one the head and shoulders have been cut off to make
a spinning bait. The needle of the spinning flight is pushed
down the centre of the body and you then have one of
the finest baits for early salmon there is.

But to return to the task of collecting sand-eels. I
usually get them just before I go fishing as they do not
stay alive long unless kept in well-oxygenated sea-water.
When boat fishing this is easy because you can place your

baits in a container with a lid on, tie a cord to it and drop it over the side, then all you have to do when you want a fresh bait is haul the container up, take one out and lower it back down again. Of course see that the cord is tied to the boat!

Even when dead fresh sand-eels make good bait for most fish when used in conjunction with drift-line, paternoster or ledger tackle.

SQUID

Obtained from most tackle shops in areas where there are sea anglers, squid without a doubt is the most versatile of all sea baits and I always try to have it on board when operating in deep water.

Most sea fish have either a highly developed sense of taste or smell, it is therefore good reasoning to surmise that any bait that gives off smell will attract. Baits that flash when moving also lure. Mackerel, herring and pilchards are good because of smell and flash, but after they have been in the water for any length of time, the skin becomes dulled and most of the smell is lost. Liver from skate or tope is an excellent lure for other predators, but once the blood smell goes it is useless. The same applies to shellfish to a lesser degree. The only way to offset these drawbacks is to change baits frequently. All the foregoing has a definite bearing on the value of squid.

In the first place every part of this mollusc is useful. Decapitated, the head is a prime bait for large bass, skate, conger and cod and no matter how long it is in the water it retains smell and flash and the tentacles waving back and forth in the current are a great attractor. The body split open together with the flap can be cut into various sizes and strips to suit the occasion. These will lure pollack, mackerel, bass, coalfish, conger, skate and even tope

Figure 48. Using a squid as bait.
1. Body and flap cut into strips.
2. Head of squid.
3. Strips of squid on hook and tied in with black nylon thread to prevent slipping.

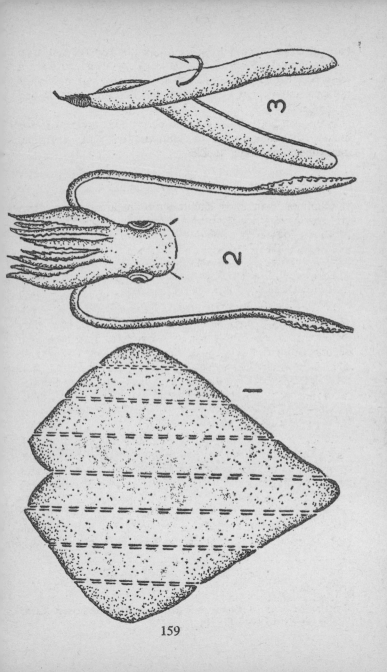

if large enough. I have had a number of 30 lb. tope on it and a couple over 40 lb.

Small narrow strips are often useful when using the baited spoon for flat fish. On occasions during every winter when rag and lugworm are difficult to come by and very often are "green" and soft. At times like these I use squid strip when after flounder.

Most anglers appreciate the value of squid as a bait for deep water work, but overlook its use when using a spoon. It has the appearance of a white worm as it is being retrieved by the angler.

In most estuaries where flounders and bass like to congregate, small crabs are also present by the score and worms are soon reduced to shreds by these voracious creatures and one needs a large supply to combat their attacks. Squid being very tough resists for a long time such attacks before a new strip is needed.

Squid is not and never will be the answer to all our bait problems, but it is a good first or second choice bait and for that reason deserves a place in everyone's bait box.

MACKEREL, HERRING AND PILCHARD

Fish flesh baits are always fairly easy to obtain, for one has only to pay a visit to the local fishmonger to purchase mackerel or herring. Pilchard is more of a west country bait. Of the first two mackerel is best being tougher in skin and flesh texture. However, herring is a very oily fish and on occasions strips of this have lured some very large fish such as cod, tope and skate. When I am using herring I also put on a strip or fillet of mackerel as well and this combination has served me very well. The year before I started to plan this book, my son had a 43 lb. tope on mackerel and herring fillets. At Deal, using this flesh-bait mixture he has had numerous 15 lb. and 20 lb. cod. Of course Deal is the home of very large cod, but I mention it to illustrate what mackerel and herring used together can do.

Cut into pieces both mackerel and herring are good paternoster and drift-line baits.

In the summer mackerel are present in most inshore waters and can be caught from beaches, piers, rocks and boats. If you can get freshly caught mackerel so much the better for the skin will have more brilliance and the flesh will have more smell. With bought fish you can never be sure how long it has been on ice. The more it is frozen the less smell it gives and the pearly sheen on the skin disappears.

Mackerel are quite easy to catch on small devons and spoons used in conjunction with your spinning rod. If fishing from a boat they can be taken in large numbers by using a trace on which there are four or six streamer flies, known in sea angling circles as "feathers". These are very easy to make with various coloured cock hackles. Four to six feathers are tied in near the eye of a No. 6 long shank sea hook. The colours which I have found to be most productive are yellow, white, blue, orange and red.

These same "feathers" are also used by some anglers to lure pollack, coalfish and cod. In the Hampshire Solent many fine pollack and cod have been caught on them when trolling.

Taking it altogether the mackerel is a most obliging sort of fish. When fresh caught it is excellent eating and it can also be used for the prime purpose of catching other fish.

12

Deep Sea Fishing

ONE of the first things I discovered about deep sea fishing, when operating from a boat, was that it has at least one thing in common with freshwater fishing and that is ground-baiting. Young anglers often fail to realise that in many cases bottom-feeding fish have to be attracted and when they become interested have to be "held" in the fishing area. So far as I am aware the only way to do this is by use of ground-bait.

I always have a couple of small sacks on board my boat and the weave of the material from which they are made is very open, allowing whatever mixture I put inside to escape in minute quantities as the sack rests on the bottom with the anchor.

The contents vary according to the fish I want to attract and eventually try to catch. In boat fishing circles a sack, bag or any type of container holding ground-bait is called a "rubby-dubby". Why such a name for ground-bait I have never been able to discover.

One of the best mixtures I have tried for such fish as pollack, cod, whiting, pout whiting, skate and conger contains half-a-dozen tins of cat food, several herrings cut into small pieces and broken up shrimps.

For bass, a mixture of herring, broken up shrimp and old ragworms that are no good for fishing with provides a good appetiser and if the hook is baited with a couple of shrimps one can expect to catch a few nice fish, particularly over shingle banks and from gullies between rocks and shingle banks.

Shrimp fragments are also excellent for use at the mouth of an estuary when sea trout are on the move, and once you have them interested in the free hand-out a small gold or silver spoon worked fairly deep will usually catch a brace or two.

Bream, both black and red, respond well to ground-baiting, but instead of shrimps they like boiled rice in liberal quantities.

Plaice, flounders and dabs are partial to chopped up lug and ragworms, mashed crabs or minced fish flesh.

In the preparation of ground-bait a friend of mine Bob Bradshaw, who has a tackle shop in Boscombe near Bournemouth and operates a charter boat for anglers has carried ground-baiting to a fine art. He uses a large mincing machine which he clamps to a seat and unwanted bait, fish, crabs, etc., are minced up on the spot. It is an excellent idea for the pieces are so small that they attract, but do not feed the fish.

Another friend does not bother with a sack even. He purchases some tins of cat food and tips their contents into a larger can with a water-tight lid. The top, bottom and sides have a lot of small holes bored in them and the can is tied on to the anchor rope a couple of feet from the anchor. To my mind this is the most simple of all methods of ground-baiting and does away with the messy job of cutting up and mixing ingredients.

RIGHT TIME TO STRIKE

The right time to strike a fish was another thing that was impressed upon me at an early age. Each and every one of the species roaming round our coasts bite differently and to be really successful one should be able to detect the species from the bite and so be able to make the proper strike.

For instance some years ago while fishing off Clare Island, County Mayo (Ireland) my boat companion was an angler from London who had never caught a tope during his 20 years of fishing. He had, he said, hooked quite a number, but they always got away.

On this particular day we ran into a school of these sharks. My companion was equipped with the best of tackle and was the first to register a bite, but judge of my surprise when a second after the fish took his mackerel fillet he struck back. Immediately his line went slack and he remarked: "It's always the same, I hit them and off they go. Why is it?"

I told him that his trouble was simply impatience. When using a single hook a tope should be allowed to run with the bait for 15 to 20 yards and the less resistance it feels the better during its initial run. It might be his last one, so be patient and let him have a good one. Therefore the check or brake should be off. Having given the fish time to get the bait well within its leathery jaws, the hook should be driven home hard.

In those days I used a single hook, today I use two hooks fastened together with wire, tandem fashion. With this tackle there is no need to wait for the tope to run, as soon as the bite is felt the strike is made and invariably the fish is hooked in the jaw with one or other of the hooks

Now compare the iron jaws of a blue shark with the soft easily-torn flesh of a grey mullet, or the great mouths of cod, whiting and bass with the tiny one of plaice. Or again, compare the nibble of a conger with the bite and run of a pollack, coalfish or mackerel.

You just cannot treat these fish alike when it comes to striking.

Let us take a closer look at the bites of some of the more common species.

Take a bass. The first indication is a solid knock, followed immediately by another one. Then comes a split second pause and away goes Mr. Bass on his run. If the strike is made on the first or second knocks it is almost a certainty he will live to fight another day. On the other hand, if the strike is delayed until a few yards have been taken from the reel drum by the fish, he should be yours for the bait is then well in his mouth or throat.

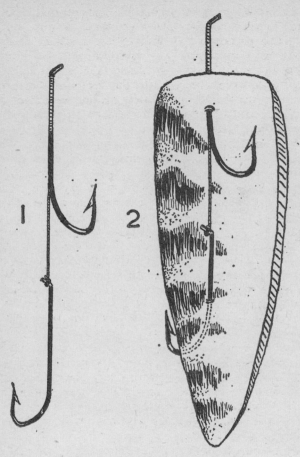

Figure 49. Pennell tackle for tope.
1. Two hooks bound together with wire.
2. A mackerel fillet impaled on the hooks.

The bite of a cod is a sudden pull and the strike should be made immediately, for the cod does not mouth a bait, but swallows it straight away. Hesitation on the part of the angler usually means a surgical operation to get the hook out.

With whiting there is no need to strike, for the fish is a glutton and invariably hooks himself. So if you are after whiting with a three-boom paternoster, when you feel the first bite, which is a sharp knock, don't reel in and his struggles will attract others of the school and your other two hooks will be tenanted as well.

The conger is a timid biter. Even one of 50 lbs. will suck and nibble at the bait several seconds before taking hold. The line will gradually tauten and then start to move off the reel. When this happens hit back hard and reel in the slack immediately and try to prevent the fish from getting back to the rock or wreck from which she came; all large congers are female. Large conger put up a terriffic fight and to allow slack line is asking for trouble.

Grey mullet also require a delayed strike after they take the bait, but while the strike should be firm it should be gentle as their lips are easily torn, even with small hooks.

So far as pollack, coalfish and mackerel are concerned, they invariably hook themselves, so vicious are their respective bites.

Plaice, flounders and dabs present little difficulty for in most cases when the bite is felt the fish has already got the bait well back in its mouth and so a tautening of the line is usually sufficient to drive home the hook. But to be on the safe side release a few feet of line and then strike.

I am convinced that it is just as important to strike at the right time as it is to use the right kind of tackle and bait. Correct timing of the strike will result in more successfuly hooked fish.

USING A DRIFT-LINE

If I were ever restricted to one form of fishing from a boat, I am fairly certain my choice would be drift-lining. It is the most simple of techniques with the bait actually "searching" for the fish. With this form of probing the deeps, one does not have to use excessive weights. When paternostering or ledgering in a strong tide, there is difficulty in holding bottom. And once a pound of lead or more goes on, most of the fun of detecting bites vanishes, to be replaced by the hard and tiresome work of reeling in, every now and then.

On a paternoster the amount of line attached to the tackle offers considerable resistance to tide or current and causes the weight to lift. The drift-line is ideally suited for strong tidal flows, fast currents and channels between deeply submerged rocks.

Tackle for drifting comprises a trace nine feet in length with Pennell tackle (two hooks) or a single hook fastened at one end, and a good class swivel at the other. Immediately above the swivel put a Jardine spiral lead. This weight is stream-lined in shape and offers less resistance to pressure. As the state of the tide or current alters it can be replaced by a lighter or heavier lead without interfering with the terminal tackle.

Experience will decide what size is best for the prevailing conditions. This also holds true for trace and line. Where there is little tide or current a 12 lb. trace and 15 lb. line is heavy enough for small cod and whiting, bass and pollack, but strong water demands strong tackle.

One of the secrets of success is the way a bait is placed on the hooks or hook. I am not big-headed enough to think my methods are the only successful ones. Far from it. But they have produced plenty of fish.

After deciding on the weight to be used, let the bait into the water and slowly release line, stopping every few yards before paying out more.

Continue until 50 or 60 yards have gone. Then put the check on and wait for a bite. Remember it often pays to recover a few yards of line every few minutes, thus keeping the bait working at different depths.

A good winter bait for cod is sprat. This is hooked on Pennell tackle, one hook near the head the other just in front of the tail. Sand-eels are good all-season baits and will take all kinds of fish, whether they be near bottom, on the bottom or near surface feeders. For sand-eels a single hook is best. The hook is put through the bottom jaw and then hooked through the loose skin near the shoulder. For skate and conger a fillet of mackerel or herring is good and so is squid, the head of which is a favourite bait of mine for thorn-back skate. With mackerel or herring bait Pennel tackle is much superior to a single hook, but with the head of a squid a single hook is sufficient, the size of the hook being dependent upon the size of the bait.

With skate, conger and tope the trace should always be of wire. Tackle shops sell traces already made up and once you have a pattern it is an easy matter to make your own. When operating over bass and pollack ground strips of mackerel or two ragworms on a single hook can be used to good effect.

A favourite bait of mine for searching the fairly shallow waters of the inshore gullies and channels is the prawn. I have caught many large bass and pollack on the bait, but it must be freshly caught. Preserved or cooked prawns can be good at times but if you want a good bag of fish take my advice and use fresh prawns. Use a single hook and impale the prawn in front of the second segment near the tail.

Another bait that accounts for most species when drift-lining is peeler or soft crab, which has been mentioned elsewhere.

A whole hermit crab, also referred to previously, is particularly deadly when fished over deep-water shingle banks. It should be impaled on a single hook through the body. Conger and skate are very partial to it. One of the largest monkfish I have ever caught, a 45-pounder when fishing at Westport (Ireland) fell to the lure of a large hermit crab, much to the surprise of the boatman for we were after skate.

KEEP HOOKS NEEDLE SHARP

Always keep your hooks needle sharp, then very little pressure is needed to drive them home. For this purpose there is nothing to beat fine emery cloth. A sheet of emery cloth size 400 is inexpensive and takes up very little room in a pocket or tackle box. The hook to be used should

168

be suitable in size for the fish and the bait. It should be efficient in its penetration and hooking power. It should be strong enough to stand the strains and struggles of a fighting fish and it should be kept in such condition that it will not corrode with the action of saltwater.

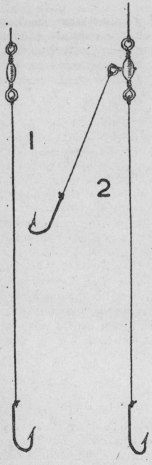

Figure 50. Drift-line tackle.
  1. Single hook.
  2. Two hooks.

A hook is a small and rather humble piece of equipment and yet it is among the most important of articles in your kit and often it is most abused by otherwise careful and methodical anglers.

You can have the most expensive rod and reel and the finest of lines, but you will still lose your fish if the hook fails you.

Hook care is frequently overlooked even by careful anglers but it is just a seemingly minor item that in turn makes those "lucky" fishermen who rarely lose fish. Take my advice and look after your hooks.

THE LEDGER AND PATERNOSTER

For bottom fishing for such species as tope, skate and conger, the ledger is a well known tackle and each season takes toll of many fine specimens. However, the use of a ledger often tends to make one a little lazy and occasionally large fish are lost together with rod, reel and tackle. No matter what kind of tackle you are using it is much safer to hold the rod than rest it against something. If you are holding the rod you can feel the bite when it comes, but if the rod is not held the first indication of a bite is a jerk of the rod-top. If it is a large fish taking the bait on the run, as it were, the rod may be pulled over the side before you can reach it.

Some anglers use two hooks on a ledger, but I much prefer one. My reason for this follows an experience I had at Deal during the cod season. It was many years ago and occurred during the month of December. My two

Figure 51. An easily made ledger tackle.

hooks were baited with mackerel fillets. I got a vicious bite and as I tightened up another fish took hold of the other hook. After a fight lasting about twenty minutes I brought both fish to the surface and as the boatman leaned over to gaff the fish on the top hook the trace broke and both fish went free. Each of those cod were in the region of 20 lbs. making a total weight of 40 lbs. which proved just too much for the trace I was using.

The ledger is a handy piece of equipment to have in readiness when using a drift-line, you find the fish with the drift-line and once located you anchor up and start fishing with a ledger.

FOR WHITING

When fishing for whiting I usually stick to the paternoster for sometimes the fish feed right on the bottom and at others feed a foot or so off the sea bed. One of the finest whiting grounds I know is located in Loch Torridon (Ross-shire) Scotland. It was from this loch that an old friend of mine Ernie Tame took his record whiting, a fish of 6 lbs.

In those days paternosters were made of brass, which old-timers used to refer to as their hard-wear. Then we had stainless steel ones and with the advent of the plastic age the booms were made of clear plastic. Today most paternosters are made of nylon monofilament, they are much lighter, take up very little room and are just as good, what is more they are very easy to make. If you have taken my advice and obtained your card from the tackle shop on how to tie knots you should experience little difficulty in tying the four loop blood knot. To the loops formed by this knot you attach your hooks which are tied to five- or six-inch lengths of nylon called snoods (see sketch).

TROLLING

This, to say the least is a lazy form of fishing but I like it particularly on a warm summer's day when fishing for mackerel or pollack and even good bags of bass have been taken with it. A spinning bait or spoon is allowed to work behind a slow-moving boat some 30 or 40 yards away.

However the secret of successful trolling is using just the right amount of lead to balance the speed of the boat for the angler's offering must be kept well down. The faster the boat goes the more lead is required to keep

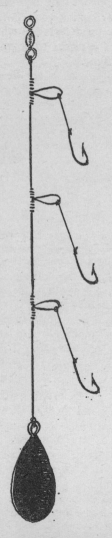

Figure 52. Nylon paternoster.

the bait down and vice versa. It is obvious that the drag on a long line when trolling is great so one needs a rod capable of standing up to the strain. The one I use is 7 ft. in length and is of solid glass. My son made it for me out of a rod kit which was purchased for £4. He also made me a heavy boat rod of solid glass from a rod kit that cost just over £4. The rings on both these rods are whipped with nylon sewing thread which I consider to be more serviceable than ordinary whipping thread.

For pollack I like a three-inch blue and silver devon armed with a treble hook, for mackerel a two-inch silver wobbling spoon or spinning spoon and for bass a natural sand-eel on spinning tackle or an artificial one like the "Mevagissey" sand-eel. In regard to mackerel I know you can get a lot more mackerel on "feathers" (streamer flies) but when you are fishing for sport and not numbers spinning a bait on the troll will give you quite a few thrills.

THE BAITED SPOON FOR PLAICE

Years ago fishing for plaice meant using ledger or drift-line tackle, then the baited spoon method was discovered. Originally the baited spoon was devised for flounder, but it was soon discovered that plaice were just as curious as flounder. It is this curiosity in the make-up of this delightful table fish that the angler exploits when using the baited spoon technique. Apparently plaice cannot resist the urge to investigate the antics of a spoon that wobbles and spins and when he sees a nice succulent lug or ragworm trailing behind he just cannot resist the urge to pick it up.

Plaice are well distributed throughout most coastal waters where there is plenty of sand and the right kinds of food. One area which is noted for its plaice fishing is Poole, Dorset. Each year without fail hundreds of thousands of plaice converge on the acres of sand flats in the area. Professional netsmen take their toll, but there always seems to be plenty left for the angler.

Now while one can fish a baited spoon from an anchored boat and catch a few fish the best method I know is drift-fishing. The tackle used is a little different to that used when after flounder. The baited-spoon is attached to a two-foot trace and this is connected to the reel line with a three-way swivel and a one or two ounce Arlesey bomb weight is tied to a six-inch length of six-pound nylon and fastened to the swivel link.

The spoon is also a little different in shape being more flattened than a flounder spoon and the pattern used at Poole is a Swedish one and called a Rauto Spoon. It is armed with a single hook (see sketch).

No casting is done. The baited spoon is lowered over the side and when the weight touches the bottom, the spoon as the fish attractor, wobbles and turns slowly as the boat drifts with the tide or current.

The Swedish spoon is fairly expensive to buy, but once you have a pattern they are fairly easy to make. The red-coloured edge round one side of the spoon can be made with the fluorescent paint used for painting the tops of freshwater floats.

I have seen some excellent plaice spoons made out of stainless steel reflectors that came from old-type car lamps picked up for a few pence at a junk-yard.

When spoon-drifting for plaice it is not an unusual thing to catch an entirely different species, twice last season I caught a brill, the last one was 4½ lbs. and made a tasty meal for my family.

As to bait, lugworm is best with ragworm a close second, but when baiting your hook see that you have a few inches hanging loose from the hook. When you get a bite ease off a few feet of line to enable the fish to get the bait well into its mouth and then tauten the line and the fish will be hooked.

TACKLE FOR BLACK AND RED BREAM

May and June are months my wife, son and I always look forward to from one year to another, the reason being that black bream are present at many places off the south coast.

This member of the bream family, however, is something of a mystery for very little is known of its habits

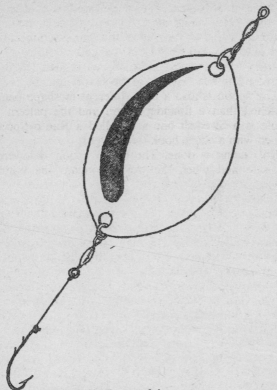

Figure 53. Rauto plaice spoon.

or life history. To procreate the species these little warriors—a four-pounder is a good one—make the long journey from the Mediterranean and when that exhausting task is done back they go.

My experience with black bream extends over many years and I have yet to meet an angler who has not been thrilled with its free-biting and gameness. It is, in my opinion, the ideal teenager's fish.

Many anglers use far too heavy tackle with the result that the fish has not a chance to show its fighting ability. Another point is that bream appreciate a free hand-out in the way of ground-bait.

For black-breaming I use a five-ounce, hollow-glass rod of seven feet in length, four-inch centre-pin reel and a line of six-pound nylon with a six-foot trace of five-pound nylon. The trace is connected to the line with a swivel. Before the line is connected to the trace a swivel is placed on the lie to run loose. On this swivel is fastened a 12-inch or 18-inch length of four-pound nylon at the end of which is fastened the weight. A glance at the accompanying sketch gives the general idea of how to fix up this tackle on which only one hook is used and a split shot is used as a stop.

The beginner might wonder at the use of only one hook, but as bream feed just above the rocks or in among the weed an additional hook can be a decided drawback under such conditions. As to baits I have taken them on small pieces of herring and mackerel, but my largest bags have always been when using small lugworm or cockle.

With such light tackle it is advisable to use a net to land your fish and the one I use has a wide mouth and a six-foot handle.

The same tackle that one uses for "blacks" is also good for the red variety. Both are excellent eating fish. Taking it all round, the black and red bream are worthy opponents for light tackle enthusiasts.

They are not so well distributed round our coasts as many other species. The best places I know for black bream include Littlehampton, Bognor, Brighton, Shoreham and right round the Devon and Cornish coastline. Red bream are more predominant in Devon and Cornwall waters than the black.

Of course no matter what kind of fish you set out to catch when operating from a boat, anchored, drifting or trolling it is odds on that you will catch other varieties and to me that is part of the fun when fishing in deep water a mile or two out from the coast. I sincerely hope that this chapter has created an urge in my readers to try it some time, but if you are under the age of 14 years try and persuade your father or an adult relative or friend to go with you just to be on the safe side.

Another point; learn to swim before you do much boat

fishing for accidents do happen. All charter boats are equipped with life-jackets or life-belts, but if you can swim as well you are well prepared for anything that might happen when you are afloat.

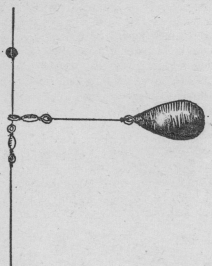

Figure 54. Flowing trace tackle for bream.

13

Beware of these fish

LIFE for most creatures of the sea is one great struggle where those who put to the best use the strength and abilities Nature has conferred upon them have, as a rule, most success. The conditions of the game are fixed, but the powers and qualities used in the struggle vary a little. Poison, spines of needle-sharpness and claws that would do justice to a carnivore together with endurance, skill and tenacity of life have their part to play, and each competitor if he hopes for success is called upon to do his best. Bearing this in mind it behoves every young angler to realise the potential dangers of certain species if handled carelessly.

On the back of my right hand is a blue and white coloured scar of three-quarters of an inch long by one eighth of an inch wide. It was inflicted more than thirty years ago by a supposedly dead sting ray, one of two twenty-pounders my father and I had taken while fishing off Deal. The boatman cut the tail off of the one my father had caught, but I wanted a photograph of the one taken by me, as it was the first large sting ray I had ever caught. The fish was given several heavy clouts on the head and for extra measure it was given a deep knife thrust between the eyes. It was then put in the fish-box.

Having got the camera set and passed over to my father

I took hold of the sting ray and had taken a couple of steps when its tail came round like a whip-lash and ripped the back of my hand. The wound was deep and bled badly, so much so that we packed up for me to get the hand attended to. Needless to say I did not get the photograph, what is more I did not return to my office for some days. Should you catch a sting ray handle it with care or you may regret it, for they hang on to life very tenaciously. They are bottom feeders and at any time when you are ledgering you may hook one.

The spur dog is another fish that needs most careful handling as each of the two dorsal fins are armed with a long claw that is needle-sharp. This particular type of dogfish when caught, bends its back into a bow and strikes backwards with terrific force, driving the claws into anything that happens to be near. A glove is no protection. The best thing to do is to put your foot on it, but not before you have killed it, then, and not before, should you try to get the hook out of its mouth. The best way to do this operation is to cut it out by slitting the side of the jaw in which it is impaled.

Most of the spur dogs I have taken have been when whiting fishing. When a school of whiting has been located the sport is usually fast and furious, but once the dogs come around your fun with the whiting will be finished and it is best to up-anchor and try and locate another school of whiting.

Occasionally when fishing for plaice, dabs, sole and flounder you might catch a little fish no more than four or five inches in length and brownish yellow in colour and covered with regular brownish lines. This is the lesser weaver or viper fish as it is often called because certain of its spines are capable of injecting poison into the wounds they make, in similar fashion to the fangs of a snake.

The spines on the dorsal fin can inflict quite a little damage to the unwary, but the most dangerous part is the head for on the upper part of the gill covers are spines which lie flat when the fish is at rest, but come out at right angles when it is alarmed. It is these that are the most dangerous for they are poisonous. They are shaped like a grooved bayonet and along these grooves the poison travels from the sacs at their base. There are at least two cases of death having been caused from the poison of this fish.

A friend of mine when scraping for sand-eels a few years ago, was incapacitated for more than a week through inadvertently catching hold of one. Within ten minutes of being stung his hand was swollen twice its normal size and he suffered much pain.

If you are fishing in weaver infested waters carry with you a little bottle of Scrubbs ammonia and should you be unfortunate enough to get stung, sponge the wound frequently with it as it will hold in check much of the inflamation and pain.

A near relative is the greater weaver, but it is not so common and much prefers deep water to shallow. In the lesser weaver the spiny dorsal has five or six spines and the greater six or more. It is a little larger and of much brighter colour, the predominating one being a brownish yellow.

The gurnard is also a species with which care should be exercised when taking it off the hook. Besides a spiked dorsal fin the whole of the head is "armour-plated" and there are some nasty dagger-pointed spines at the edges of the gill covers. Unless the hands are gloved it is best to put a foot on the fish while the hook is being extricated.

Incidentally, a pair of leather gloves is also handy when bass fishing as I mentioned in another chapter.

During the summer it is not unusual for the south and west coastal waters to be invaded by thousands of jelly-fish. Should the line or tackle come into contact with them the streamers of the jelly-fish will wrap themselves round and you then have the unpleasant task of cleaning them off. Do not clean your tackle with the bare hands for the results will be anything but pleasant, especially if you touch your face or arms afterwards. Gloved hands and a piece of rag are the safety precautions to take in jelly-fish infested waters.

The conger-eel is also a fish the novice should treat

180

with care, its jaws are powerful with teeth sharp and dangerous. Before ever you set about the task of removing the hook make sure that it is dead. Far better cut the tackle and mount another one than take the risk of being bitten.

14

Sea Angling home-work

My father was often in the habit of declaring "For the angler there is never a wasted day". By that he meant when one could not fish due to climatic conditions or other reasons there was always plenty to do, this he designated as "home-work".

When the sea goes on a rampage, hurling gigantic waves hither and thither as if they had no more weight than feathers, the saltwater enthusiast can spend a profitable hour or two, renewing this and that piece of tackle or making up something new.

Sometimes natural bait is hard to come by, but if one has a supply of artificials, sport can still be enjoyed among the near-surface feeders such as bass, mackerel, pollack and coalfish. Once you have caught a fish then you have some fish-flesh for the bottom feeders.

Figure 55. How to make mackerel and pollack spinners.
1. Length of stainless steel or brass wire.
2. Small split ring.
3. Length of brass or copper tubing.
4. Two red beads.
5. Spinner of copper or brass is cut to shape and tubing soldered on.
6. Finished spinner with long cock hackles tied on hook.
7. Long-bladed spinner with long-shanked hook.

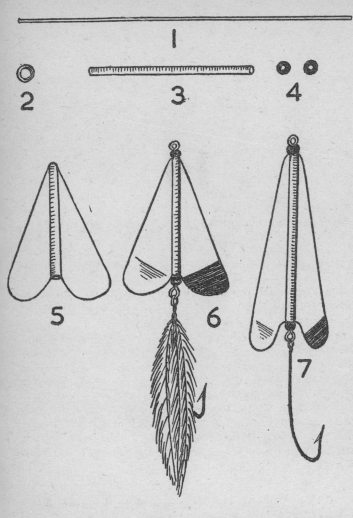

1

2 3 4

5 6 7

Some years ago while on holiday at Shieldaig, Ross-shire (Scotland) I had set off to do some spinning from the rocks and caught a ten-inch pollack. It was hooked in the throat and was bleeding badly so had to be killed and rather than leave the fish to be eaten by the gulls I cut it down through the middle and made a couple of nice bottom baits. Fixing up a ledger I cast one out and caught a 15 lb. common skate on it. The other half of the pollack was taken not by a fish, but by a two-pound crab which I managed to land with my long-handled net. It made a lovely lunch for two of us.

Mackerel and pollack spoons are fairly easy to make from sheet brass or copper. When made you can tin them over to make them a silver colour or give them a high polish and leave them in their natural colour.

A look at the accompanying sketches will show you what materials are needed and how to fit them together. You will notice in sketches No. 6 and 7 the finished spoons have single hooks. Mackerel spoons you purchase have treble hooks attached, but having tried both treble and single hooks, I much prefer the single, as it bites much deeper and there is no chance of one hook acting as a lever against another. Single hooks should be No. 6 long-shank with straight eye.

Each of the two spoons I have referred to have split rings to which the hook is attached, this enables one to change a hook quite easily. For instance you may want to put on a streamer fly as in sketch No. 6, with the split ring it is easy. Spoons sold in tackle shops are minus the split ring so if the hook loses a barb or is otherwise damaged you have the job of taking the spoon apart to put on another hook, it also means you will have to make another shank for the spoon.

CLIPS FOR WEIGHTS

You can make quite a few things with brass and stainless steel wire. For boat fishing, clips are needed to hold your weights when bottom fishing. The clips in the accompanying illustration are very easy to make, what is more their design enables one to change weights quite easily. Besides a pair of pliers to cut the wire you will need a pair of round-nose pliers to shape the clips.

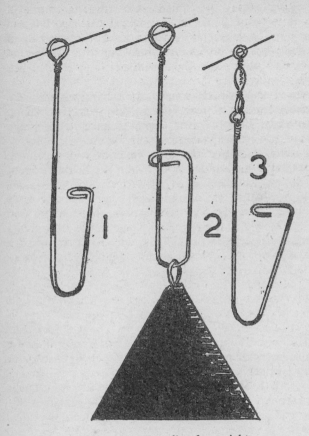

Figure 56. Wire clips for weights.
1. Brass or stainless steel clip for weight.
2. Clip with weight attached.
3. Clip in which a swivel is included.

EASY TO MAKE WIRE TRACE

For bottom feeding fish with powerful jaws and teeth one has to use a wire trace and a glance at the sketch shows how easy they are to make. I always have several made up whenever I am going after such species as conger-eel, skate and tope. All you need are two barrel swivels and a link-swivel. The line is fastened to the end barrel swivel and the hook to the link-swivel. The wire I use mostly in traces is Alasticum which you can purchase in strengths of from a few pounds right up to 100 pounds breaking strain.

A friend of mine who does a lot of shark fishing in Ireland every year uses traces of 100 pounds. The beauty of this type of wire is that it does not kink very easily and being pliable is easily straightened. In the old days we made our traces out of wire gimp which was not so serviceable in that being composed of a number of fine strands, it broke fairly easily once the strands became worn. Indeed, my wife once lost a very big conger-eel, when fishing over a wreck at Torbay (Devon) through her gimp trace breaking.

Of course there are other kinds of wire to be had such as plastic-coated, cable-laid, etc., but if you stick to Alasticum you won't go far wrong.

PERSPEX BOOM

This type of boom is very handy to have, it does not take up much room and can be used to make up a paternoster, a ledger or can be used with a long flowing trace when one is fishing on the drift, or fishing from the beach.

Perspex cut-offs can be purchased at most handycraft stores, and pieces one-eighth-of-inch thickness are ideal. The width of the booms I use are half-inch and the length from three to six inches. This man-made material is easy to cut with a hack-saw and can be shaped with a file. A hole is bored as per sketch and should be just large enough to allow the stainless steel or brass wire link to move round easily. Another hole is bored, as in sketch, and to this is attached the hook tackle. A flowing trace can be anything in length from five to nine feet, but if you intend making two or three booms, up into a paternoster, then length of nylon from boom to hook—called a snood —will be from four to six inches in length.

Figure 57. An easy made wire trace.
1. Barrel swivel.
2. Barrel swivel.
3. Link swivel for attaching hook.

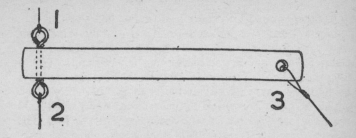

Figure 58. Perspex boom.
1. Line to reel.
2. Line to weight.
3. Trace to hook.

RUBBER RAGWORM

Another little item one can make quite easily at home is a rubber ragworm. About 50 years ago they were in common use all over the country, but like the rubber sand-eel they have been replaced by plastic ones. However, having used both types I can say with confidence that the ones of rubber are much superior to plastic ones. Here then is how to make a rubber ragworm.

An old inner, red colour, tube of a motor-car will provide enough material to make dozens. Two pieces, five inches long by half-inch wide are cut out with about 30 pieces $\frac{1}{16}$ inch wide by three-quarters-inch long from a new red (cycle) tyre repair patch. These are stuck on to one of the larger pieces with solution to represent the appendages of the ragworm, a long-shanked hook is placed in position and the next piece of tubing is stuck on top with rubber solution.

When set, stitch round the hook with red-coloured nylon sewing thread and bind in the head with the same kind of thread leaving the eye of the hook protruding to which you can fasten your line. You now have a bait that has accounted for flat-fish, such as plaice and flounder and also bass and pollack.

188

Another simple rubber bait to make is known as the "Sarcelle" and was much in evidence on the south and west coasts many years ago. It consists of a rubber ring taken from a one-pound preserving jar lid, and a No. 6 long-shank hook. The rubber ring, washer I suppose would be a better name, is cut in half and the two pieces are whipped onto the hook. For trolling when bass and mackerel are about it can be most effective. At Peel, Isle of Man some years ago I had 33 mackerel in one morning's fishing with it.

So much for making up tackle and baits. We now turn to care of tackle once more. Whenever you have a blank period take a look at your rod and reel. Modern fibreglass rods with their stainless steel rings need little attention, but occasionally one finds a ring-whipping becoming frayed. When this happens renew it at once.

Your reel should be cleaned and oiled whenever it has been used, never let it go too long without attention, or else, one day it will go on strike.

In conclusion, I hope that YOU the angling experts of the future have enjoyed the reading as much as I have the writing. May we all hook a good one on our next outing.

INDEX

The use of et seq in this index shows that the discussion of the subject runs on to the next few pages.

A

Alasticum   62, 185
Artificial baits   116

B

Baited spoon   173
Baiting with maggots   33
Baits   150 et seq
Balsa wood baits   119
Balsa wood plugs   120
Barbel   20, 26, 53
Bass   145, 146
Black ghost   133
Bleak   27
Blood knot   86
Blue charm salmon fly   136, 137
Bottom fishing   55
Bread-paste   26, 37, 31
Bream   20, 45, 162, 174, 175, 176
Brill   175
Brown and gold devon minnow   64

C

Caddis grub   96, 97
Carp   28, 48, 49, 50
Carp baits   50
Casting   32, 83, 90
Chub   20, 26, 36, 42, 43, 44, 45
Chub flies   42
"Clean" salmon   110
Clips for weights   184
Cockles   152, 153
Cod   162, 165
Colorado spoon   64, 65
Common bream   28
Common limpet   155
Conger   162, 165, 180, 181
Cork floats   18
Crabs   155
Crystal hook   20

D

Dace   20, 27, 50
Dangerous fish   178
Deep sea fishing   162 et seq
Devon   36, 117
Drift-line tackle   169
Drift-lining   166
Dry-fly   91, 124
Dry-fly rods   80
Dye for maggots   44

E

Early season fishing   113, 114
Eel   27
Elder pith floats   18
Estuary fishing   143
Eyed hook   20

F

Finnish lure   73
Fishing at night   102
Fixed spool reel   15

Flies   51, 81 et seq, 103-107
Float-cap   18
Float fishing   30
Float-making   17, 20
Float tackle   36
Floats   15, 46, 51, 53
Flounder   148
Flounder spoon   148, 149
Fly dressing   128 et seq
Fly fishing   42, 51
Fly fishing tackle   80
Fly patterns   104
Foul-hooked   124
Freshwater shrimp   96, 97

G

Gaff   112, 113
Good fishing weather   141
"Grasshopper"   72, 73
Grayling   27, 69
Grayling float   71
Grayling season   70
Ground baiting   30
Gudgeon   20, 24, 27
Gurnard   180

H

Hackled flies   82
Hair-winged dry fly   135, 136
Hair-winged wet fly   134
"Hatch" of flies   92
Haunts   22, 23
Herring   160
Hempseed   24
Hermit crab   155
Hollow-glass rod   15
Hooks   20, 168
Hook sizes   20

I

Insect colouration   89
Inshore water fish   142

J

Jam jar minnow trap   38, 39
Jelly fish   180
Jetties   140

K

Keep net   33
"King" carp   50
Knots   112

L

Lake fishing   90
Large pike   57
Leaders   81, 84
Leather carp   50
Ledgering   34, 44, 45, 57, 66, 145, 146, 170
Lesser weaver   179
Lines   80, 81

190

Live baiting 57, 66
Long distance casting 58
Long-trotting 50
Lugworm 150

M

Mackerel 160
Mackerel and pollack spinners 182, 183
Maggots 24, 26, 27, 33, 71, 101
Mallard and claret 132
March brown 130, 131
Minnow 24, 36, 38, 96, 98
Mirror carp 50
Mullet 144, 165
Mussel 152

N

Natural baits 96, 97, 114
  mounting of 115
"Naturals" 94
Nature's sign post 76
Net 113
Nymph 24, 70, 89, 93

O

Observation 12
"Otter" 117, 118
Overnight ground bait 45

P

Palmers 42, 43
Paternoster 39, 66
Patience 11
Pennell Tackle 95, 167
Perch 20, 24, 36
Perch paternoster 35
Perspex boom 186, 188
Pike 20, 28, 56 et seq
Pike bait 61
Pike fishing tackle 59
Pike rod 58
Pilchard 160
Plaice 173
Playing a salmon 116
Plug fishing 57, 62, 63
Plumbing the depth 31
Pollack 162, 173
Prawns 155, 156, 168
Preserved prawn 120

Q

Quill-bodied flies 92
Quill minnow 40-42

R

Rag worm 150
Reel 15, 81, 111
Removing hooks 61, 133
Roach 20, 24
Rods 14
Round-bent hooks 20
Rubber rag worm 188
"Rubby-dubby" 162
Rudd 20, 24, 51, 52

S

Salmon 109 et seq, 144
Salmon flies 122
Sand eels 156
"Sarcelle" 189
Sea angling 137 et seq
Sea trout 99 et seq
Semi-underwater plugs 62
Sharp bends 78
Shell fish 151
"Shooting" the line 84
Shrimps 155
Silver wobbling spoon 64, 65
"Sink and draw" 72
Skate 162
Slipper limpet 153, 154
Small red worm 71
Snood 187
Spade end hooks 20
Spiders 82, 129 et seq
Spinners 40
Spinning 57, 64, 98, 114
Spinning baits 62
Split shots 20, 32
Spoon and worm combination 25
Spoons 57, 116, 117, 148, 149, 184
Sprats 114, 167
Spur dog 179
Squid 158
Sting ray 178, 179
Streamer 103
Striking 40, 46, 60, 70, 90, 92, 96,
           111, 164 et seq
"Swan shots" 34

T

Tackle 14, 106, 142
Tailer 113
Teasing 62, 63
Tench 26, 46, 47
"The Test" 121
Tide rips 140
Tides 140, 141, 143
Tope 163, 164
Touch ledgering 34
Trolling 171, 172
Trotting 70
Trout 76 et seq
Trout lines 81
Turle Knot 85

V

Viper fish 179

W

Water snail 47
Waves 139
Wet flies 88
Wet fly rods 80
Whiting 162, 165, 171
Wine bottle minnow trap 37
Winged flies 82
Winter chub fishing 44
Wire trace 185, 187
Working a fly 123
Worm 24, 26, 27, 38, 44, 45, 94, 100
Worm farm 74, 99